Science and
Our Troubled Conscience

Science
and Our
Troubled
Conscience

J. ROBERT NELSON

FORTRESS PRESS   Philadelphia

Library of Congress Cataloging in Publication Data

Nelson, J Robert, 1920–
   Science and our troubled conscience.

   1. Religion and science—1946–   I. Title.
BL240.2.N44   261.5'5   80–8045
ISBN 0–8006–1398–8

8527F80   Printed in the United States of America   1–1398

To My Scientist Son
Eric Mercer Nelson

Contents

Preface

The messages people write in guest books are usually conventional but sometimes cryptic. A strange statement appears in the book of the Indian Institute of World Culture in Bangalore: "I have been a missionary for three extinct religions." It is signed by the geneticist, J. B. S. Haldane. His friends who survive him might know which three religions he meant. But it is a safe guess that Science was not one of them; for Science as a virtual religion is by no means extinct. It reproduces, evolves, mutates, and makes quantum leaps forward. It relates micro-revelations and macro-revelations, and its promises of salvation for many human ills are credible because so many have already been fulfilled. The professional hierarchy—priesthood, novices, and laity—of Science is great in number and found everywhere. Its ecumenical movement recognizes no national or linguistic barriers, although politics strain working relations. And its saints are canonized annually in Stockholm.

The great domed temple of the Massachusetts Institute of Technology is a sacred place for Science. To it were invited in 1979 many representatives of another nonextinct religion, Christianity. How the World Council of Churches Conference on "Faith, Science and the Future" came to be hosted by M.I.T. is a symptom of a new development which would have baffled the late Dr. Haldane.

Scientists did not invite church people to come and be overwhelmed by their dazzling knowledge and technical achievements. Nor did churches respond with the intention of converting the devotees of the new religion to the old. The event was unprecedented. Hundreds of persons—mostly scientists themselves as well as Christians—came from every continent. Social scientists, people of public service, theologians, and many graduate students also participated. A few spoke for religions other than Christian.

Each day they had meals in the presence of an ironically amusing but provocative mural in the dining room of the Francis Amasa Walker Memorial Building. The muralist, Edwin H. Blashfield, in 1930 had taken the story of the Temptation of Adam and Eve as the model for his theme of the omniscience and omnicompetence of Science. In place of Adam there stands the white-coated scientist. Gathered below his feet and looking up with reverent respect are a student, officers of the army and navy, and one who is either an executive or statesman. They watch as a robed figure (Wisdom?) crowns the scientist, her words being inscribed below. The old Latin gives the story a significant change: "You will be like gods [not the biblical God], knowing good and evil." There is no serpent, however, because here there is no temptation. It is the coronation of the scientist-king, who possesses not only knowledge but the ethical discernment of good and evil. The theory of "value-free science" had not commended itself to the artist.

Christianity has much to say about good and evil, too. It is "value-laden" in the extreme. But its contemporary theologians and interpreters of ethics are by no means confident of their own ability, or the church's, to look at the numerous personal and social problems of science-based technology and pronounce, "Thus saith the Lord."

Science and religious faith need each other. For many in either category, this statement is wholly unacceptable. For many others it is a truism, almost a banality. What binds the two dimensions together is simply the present precarious condition of the human race (precarious meaning literally "to be prayed for").

To work out the implications of that affirmation of mutual need, the program of study on Church and Society of the World Council of Churches* has devoted nearly a decade to research and consultation. The conference at M.I.T. was the culmination of that effort but not its completion. In fact, as the conference report reveals, new and urgently important issues have been placed on the agenda for continuing investigation. The conference has done more than fill the docket with more

---

*The World Council of Churches is the organization in which nearly three hundred Protestant and Eastern Orthodox churches express their unity in common efforts of importance to all Christians and to all human beings.

problems, however. It has set a new standard of cooperation between professional scientists and theologians, and various kinds of persons who bear responsibilities in education, politics, and society.

One of the leading and most dedicated participants in the Church and Society sub-unit of the Council was the noted anthropologist, Dr. Margaret Mead. In the last years of her life, she found occasions to emphasize her strongest conviction, expressed in her phrase: Toward a *human* science. Equally at home and respected in scientific associations and churches, Margaret Mead was prophesying what might happen at M.I.T. It was the discovery of mutuality in the concern for a human society characterized by justice for all, responsible participation in major social decisions, and sustaining an earthly environment and human environment for the good of all.

This book is the effort of one who shares her conviction. It is neither by intention nor in fact a conference report. Materials from the body of documentation have been freely used, however, along with books, articles, and other relevant writings. It is one person's interpretation of some of the major problems with which the delegates struggled during two weeks in July.

Much is said today of "contextuality" of theological and ethical thinking. That usually implies the context of political and social tensions over human rights, equity of economic opportunity, and liberation from "oppressive power structures" in many countries. While keeping sensitively aware of this ferment in contemporary history, I have tried to clarify the insights of faith and ethics in the particular context of onrushing developments in science and technology. Since it is by our daily experience with technology that we are led to an encounter with the theories and methods of diverse sciences, the book begins with that experience.

The persons to whom I am indebted for encouragement and assistance are many, but I wish to mention a few especially. It was through the good offices of Dr. Paul Abrecht, Director of the World Council of Churches' sub-unit on Church and Society, that I was co-opted as a staff member of the M.I.T. conference. During a sabbatical leave, I enjoyed the favor of being a scholar of the Joseph and Rose Kennedy Institute of Ethics at Georgetown University. The late director of the Institute, André Hellegers, M.D., had first invited me to the prestigious center of study, but his untimely death deprived me of the personal association I had so warmly anticipated. However, to the Institute's acting director, Dr. Richard A. McCormick, S.J., and his staff I owe sincere thanks for numerous courtesies, and to the Joseph P. Kennedy, Jr. Foundation for enabling support.

It was also my good fortune during the sojourn in Washington, D.C., to be visiting scholar at the College of Preachers of the Washington Cathedral upon the gracious invitation of Dr. Clement W. Welsh and Dr. Earl H. Brill. To paraphrase a word of St. Paul, I have been debtor to both Catholic and Episcopalian.

Finally, to Norman Hjelm I express appreciation for making all arrangements for the publication of this book by the Fortress Press, of which he is the Director.

Washington, D.C.
February 1, 1980

Science and
Our Troubled Conscience

1 | Technology's Ambiguous Good and Uncertain Future

"ON THE THRESHOLD OF SELF-TRANSFIGURATION"

Reflecting on the transiency of human existence is probably as old as the experience of self-consciousness. It is the occasion for saying anxious prayers, erecting supposedly perpetual memorials to the dead, shaping sad songs and melancholy verses, indulging in careless debaucheries, or simply gazing at the stars on a dark, clear night. The brief cycles of seedtime and harvest, of monsoons and droughts, of freezing and thawing have always measured the passing moments of one's lifetime. Before people became permanently confined to their urban prisons of cement and asphalt, they marked the shifting of constellations, the return of migratory birds, the sprouting buds and browning leaves. But everywhere, in city, country, or wilderness, are seen the ongoing events of birth and death, of bright beginnings and early endings.

While each person's existence seems short, however, the eras of geological and human history are awesomely long. The mystique of a millennium has always fascinated the wondering mind of sage and chronicler. Changes between generations, and even between centuries, were until recently relatively minor. Dynasties which managed to keep thrones for two or three centuries did indeed see major transformations of agricultural and military methods, styles of dress and architecture, modes of writing, and routes of commercial trade and conquest. But it was the millennium which signified the significant turning of time's wheel or the attainment of critical stages of man's pilgrimage through history.

With similar lentitude the progress of scientific discovery and tech-

1

nical invention extended slowly over the centuries from the dawn of civilization to the seventeenth century of the Christian calendar. Each civilization made its contribution to the converging streams which were to become the single broad and turbulent river of science-based technology. Various histories of science record the precocious theories of Greeks, Chinese, and Arabs, as well as the prodigious engineering feats of Egyptians, Indians, and Romans. Their ancient models of physical movement and construction, and their theories of how natural phenomena occur, endured until the sixteenth century in Europe. Then, suddenly, the pace of research, discovery, invention, and communication quickened. The *renaissance* of old knowledge and technique merged with the *naissance* of the new and unexpected. Under pressure which increased exponentially in power, there was an acceleration of concerted thought, accumulating knowledge, and industrial skill. Just as the great sluggish courses of Africa's Blue and White Niles are forced to flow between the walls of narrow ravines and plunge over steep cliffs, so the power of scientific thought and technique was compressed during the nineteenth century. What had previously been regarded as progress in the course of the centuries became the changes of mere decades or less. As Thomas A. Edison, in 1879, gave the human race its small glass globe for turning nightdark into daylight, the mental activity of the whole race seemed to become almost incandescent and luminous, shining like a ring of thought—observed a Jesuit scientist—a noösphere enveloping the whole earth.

In the intensified thought of millions there was a building up of explosive power. When the moment of detonation came, it would blast away many of the seemingly stable structures of scientific thought and technical achievement which had stood for generations and centuries. The force of explosion was felt—quite literally—at Los Alamos, New Mexico, in 1945. A second blast came at virtually the same time when the first electronic computer, Mark I, went into action. And yet a third shock occurred at Cambridge, England in 1953 when the genetic cryptograph of the omnipresent DNA molecule was first decoded.

Within eight years began three new eras of human cunning: atomic, cybernetic, and microbiological. Day by day in subsequent years newly patented inventions and formulas have been appropriated by industries large and small for the prodigal production of materials, machines, and processes. It is understandable why every essay and book on the present proliferating quantity of scientific theory and technological production must, like this one, struggle to find language adequate to express the facts. It was no exercise in futuristic hyperbole when Georgetown University political scientist Victor C. Ferkiss wrote in 1968:

> Humanity today is on the threshold of self-transfiguration, of attaining new powers over itself and its environment that can alter its nature as fundamentally as walking upright or the use of tools.[1]

If such be the point to which we as a civilized humanity are coming, are we to greet the advent with enthusiastic joy, doubtful hesitancy, or grave apprehension? In the industrially and economically developed countries, as well as in the wealthy developing ones, people already know the goods and evils which technology can bring. Are they prepared to accept with equanimity the inevitable onrush of life-changing devices and systems?

Commenting with disapproval, the respected philosopher of culture, Lewis Mumford, wrote about the rapid rise of technical civilization:

> The chief premise common to both technology and science is the notion that there are no desirable limits to the increase of knowledge, of material goods, of environmental control; that quantitative productivity is an end in itself, and that every means should be used to further expansion.[2]

Whether this premise should be accepted, honored, rejected, opposed or just ignored fatalistically is the question at the root of our present quandary. With only a slight knowledge of Greek, one can fashion many English words from *tekhné,* and their shades of meaning readily make sense: *technology,* the whole field of development of devices, machines, and systems based upon scientific reflection and research; *technique* (or *technic*), the minor components of technology (such is the distinction drawn and used by the Organization for Economic Co-operation and Development); *technocracy,* the power of technology used to rule and dominate other people; *technophilia,* the love of it; *technophobia,* the dread of it; *technolatry,* the worship of it; *technomancy,* the alleged magic of all that are called "wonders" of technology.

Science is called pure science when it is an intellectual, experimental investigation of phenomena not yet, or poorly, understood. It is unencumbered by the expectation or necessity of being practical. But, like active chemicals, scientific effort cannot remain in a pure state very long. From the laboratory investigator's cry of "Eureka!" to the advertiser's insistent pitch "Buy this product!" is usually a short space of time. While scientific research and practical application permeate the social sphere of economics and politics, most of us encounter them primarily in the materials and things produced as the result of discoveries and inventions.

Only a mind virtually devoid of the inclination or capacity to be reflective and critical can be oblivious to the problematic values of today's burgeoning volume of science and technology and their techniques. Their effects upon individuals and society are so evident and so ambiguous that one has to take a position, define an attitude, or at least have a perspective on them.

Behind every plate of food on the table, delivery of fuel, machine of production or convenience, tax statement or electronic mode of entertainment there is a quantum of injustice, deprivation, and suffering: someone's ill-paid labor, some environmental damage, some waste of energy, some policy by which human resources are wrongly allocated, exploited, or rewarded. Daily experience is so fully affected by technology derived from science that none but the hermit can escape the moral involvement of being a dependent consumer. Since my consumption inevitably means some other person's loss as well as someone's profit, the ways in which technology is used must impinge, however faintly, upon my conscience. No wonder that mine is a troubled conscience, stricken by my thoughts of the uncertain good and the ambiguous future of our increasingly technological culture.

BETWEEN SUBSISTENCE AND SURFEIT

To declare oneself wholly opposed to science and technology is either a self-deceiving romanticism or a kind of madness. Human life requires technology as much as daily food. The people who lived only by hunting and gathering food demonstrated the indispensability of invention. A pointed stick or a blunt club extended a hunter's power to kill game. A sharpened stone enabled him to cut trees for huts, and a tree made to fall across a stream became a bridge. From the mortar and pestle to the wheel and axle, technological advancement has kept adding to the mechanical necessities by which people live.

We can appreciate personally the irreplaceable value of technological devices by imagining a full day's experiences without them. In the life pattern of anyone who might read these pages, what things are dispensable and what are essential? Perhaps only the air we breathe is available without the mediation of human skill and some kind of construction. Even the conveyance of water and the supply of food, our minimal necessities, require the use of invented techniques. From there upward rises a scale of countless degrees of utility and dispensability. The question at the bottom is "What can you do without?" At the top is asked, "What do you still desire?"

The questions simply express the perennial condition of human existence between subsistence and surplus, between survival and surfeit. The symbol of the satisfaction of material needs and desires is the marketplace. The connotation of "market" and the mental image it suggests is the fecundity of production and the lure of a limitless variety of goods.

Two markets existing today can symbolize the extremes of the scale of necessities and wants. One displays the products of a pretechnological culture; the other of what we consider—at least for now—to be advanced technology.

The first is in Ethiopia, on a three-acre plateau down the hill from the city of Lalibela. Ten thousand people live here in stark simplicity. Nearly a thousand years ago, their ancestors had achieved a technical wonder. On directions from an angel, King Lalibela initiated the construction of a new Jerusalem. Along with his "Mount of Olives" and "River Kidron" he had ten monolithic churches, full size, cut from the soft massive rock on which the city stands. Without a trace of masonry, the churches have remained through centuries, but they were not seen by foreign visitors until some Portuguese came in the sixteenth century. Today one comes by small airplane and Land Rover to the remote town. On a Saturday morning the visitor wants to see the weekly market, eager to find rare and unusual articles at bargain prices. Descending toward the tableland, he may pass Lalibela's only bank: an outdoor stall, with two men seated on the earth and protecting small stacks of coins. At the marketplace, vendors have spread their wares. Some have

5

walked for five hours over mountain paths to make small transactions. But what does the foreign shopper see in the simple booths or on ragged ground cloths? Dried goat skins, red seed corn, green peppers, potatoes, firewood and charcoal. Two or three sellers offer bolts of calico cotton, imported and transported from great distance. But that is all. Where are the woven woolen rugs, rich embroideries, metal tools, works of brass and silver, products of art and craft? One must go south, several days journey on foot, to the great market of Addis Ababa. For the people of Lalibela it might as well be in Rome or Bombay. Theirs is the simple life, unencumbered by those expensive burdens of technological production against which romantic Europeans and Americans declaim. If one has goat skins and charcoal, what more could one desire?

The symbol of technology's triumph in manufacturing and commerce could be any great department store or trade fair of an industrial country, but perhaps the best expression is that great store-city, the bargain center of the world: tax-free Hong Kong. Textiles, televisions, watches, typewriters, cameras, marine motors, cars of all makes, electrical gadgets and electronic devices, heavy machinery, computers— "You name it, we have it, or we can get it for you." If it is not in the showroom or on the shelf, any one of thousands of manufactured articles can be ordered by reference to catalogs and dealers who represent many countries. If it is true that human avarice, having once been stimulated by knowledge of accessible possessions, is insatiable, then the agents and merchants of all the factories and Hong Kongs of the world keep feeding that desire. Like Goethe's oft mentioned sorcerer's apprentice with the endless buckets of water, industries, great and small, pour out such floods of merchandise that inventories must be reduced periodically by drastic clearance sales to make room for incoming shipments. In their zeal for new designs and more profits, some manufacturers plan their products to be obsolescent; they then use the power of psychologically cogent advertising to persuade customers to replace the partly worn for the new article. Indeed, the supercharged technology in its commercial expression calls people not human beings, but simply customers, consumers, or the market. So it is not always fair or reasonable to hold individual persons responsible for their addiction to consumerism and their consequent inability to distinguish between things they need and things without which they could live.

If the choice for each person were just between Lalibela and Hong Kong, few except the devotees of strict asceticism would choose the former. The true choices are not so categorical, however. On that scale of necessity and dispensability, most people living in the technically developed countries have come to depend upon, and take for granted, the products and services which for masses in other lands are regarded as unattainable luxuries: plumbing, electricity, heating and cooling systems, telephones, phonographs, television, motor cars, processed and packaged food, fresh milk, medical and dental service, banking, insurance, books and daily papers. These are called the blessings of technology which people can use and enjoy individually. But there are, of course, myriad other benefits of a civil and social kind: subway systems, movies, highways, airlines, sewage plants, bridges, printing plants, and factories, factories, factories.

The use or possession of such amenities is now considered normal and necessary for a large, but still minority, part of the world's population. Due to the current revolution of rising expectations, they are also within the range of the same and feasible desire of many other people of the world. If Danes have home refrigerators, why not Indonesians? If Italy has a national airline, why not Ghana?

We need only these few reminders that our lives are dependent upon many of the machines and devices engendered by the two kinds of technology. The first kind is the technology of simple, practical invention, constantly developing since prehistoric human experience. It still continues in the present era without much reference to science, as human ingenuity contrives tools and mechanical articles. The other is science-based technology, a recent phenomenon. It began in the latter time of the eighteenth-century industrial revolution, principally in England. Before then, scientific research was primarily a quest for understanding the workings of nature and human life: it was mainly an effort of philosophers or a hobby of wealthy aristocrats. As research moved into the laboratories of universities and industrial firms, science became the spearhead (an archaic term!) or nose cone of new invention and technological development. So the two kinds coexist today.[3] The former produced the candle, and the latter the electric light—but both are indispensable, since even in the best of technological societies the electricity supply may fail.

Dependency in itself is not always to be deplored, as the rhetoric of those who speak strongly against technology implies. If dangers to human integrity are attributed to technology and dependence upon its products, some careful distinctions must be made to prevent the criticism from being merely ridiculous. There can be no dentist, ophthalmologist, or surgeon without fine instruments and machines, no plumber without tools (which, proverbially, he forgets to bring along), no journalist without typewriter and telephone. Such a list can be endless, since every occupation has its necessary tools and accessories. That is a kind of dependency which none can sensibly criticize. On greater scale, too, every productive farm, manufacturing firm, opera company, airline, and university depends on numerous articles and services provided by science-based technology. Still greater, the space exploration program of a nation or the concerted effort to maintain an up-to-date military system depends upon a quantity of scientific research, invention, and technical development which defies comprehension.

HOW DO THINGS WORK?

Ignorance and mystification about many technical systems and devices characterize the people who are the buyers, users, and consumers of them. This is an inevitable but ironic concomitant of the technological revolution. Few people were puzzled or perplexed by the useful objects of prescientific times. One had no need to understand the complicated chemistry of a candle or oil lamp: it was only a matter of lighting it. Anyone with a modest gift of perceiving how mechanical things are related could analyze the operation of a door lock, a brake on the wagon wheels, or a water pump by the kitchen sink. A simple lesson in optics could teach one to understand the telescope and microscope, burning glass or reading glass. The steam-driven piston in rudimentary form presented no baffling problem to one's intelligence.

Since the outbreak in this century of automobile production and the proliferation of electrical and electronic devices, appliances, and systems, however, millions of people have a diminishing comprehension of the machines they use or of the mechanical systems to which they are daily subjected. Service and repair have become big business, big headaches, and big items in one's personal budget. Many men and women are no more knowledgeable about the actual functioning of a television set than are their small children, who nevertheless know precisely how to turn it on and find the channel they have learned to want. The car won't start, the vacuum cleaner is dead, the turntable doesn't turn, the toaster won't pop toast, the digital wristwatch needs repair—all these familiar crises in a middle-class household provoke people to feel frustration, anger, and helplessness.

Apart from their inability to repair things, they can only gawk at the sophisticated machines which do function well. Since their introductions only a few years ago, these have become an accepted part of daily life in the industrialized societies. People see things happen which are totally beyond comprehension, they hear of even greater wonders, and quickly accept them into their pattern of living.

Why all those black lines on packages and labels? The clerk passes pickle jars, frozen beans, and packages of biscuits over a tiny window on the counter. Nothing seems to happen—except that a constant inventory of each commodity is being kept by some seeing, unseen computer.

A woman approaches the airline counter and asks for the ticket she has reserved. The clerk types a few keys and the computer goes into action. Name and flight plans appear on the screen. The typewriter begins clacking in response to no visible fingers, the little sphere bearing the type of alphabet and numeral is spinning faster than the eye can follow. Click, click, and the perfectly typed ticket appears, with a window-seat reservation in the no-smoking section. The first few times she sees this phenomenon, the passenger is dazzled and baffled. Soon, if she travels much, it seems no more interesting than the old method of ticket issuance by telephone and handwriting.

She cannot begin to understand how her huge jet plane will be brought down through darkness and fog to a safe landing by an automatic ground control. Or how microelectronic chips of printed circuits —getting smaller and cheaper by the year—actually enable the small, thin calculator in her purse to add, multiply, and remember numbers.

Or how the success of her brother's brain surgery was made possible by laser beams. Or how the space satellite, 22,000 miles up, transmits instantly television programs from any part of the world. Or how microbiologists modify those much-publicized DNA molecules—three feet long yet too small to be seen—so that the genetic code for cell building can determine the formation of new kinds of living tissue.

Automation has taken over the issuing of her bills, sorting her mail, and processing her checks at the bank. At her hospital or health maintenance organization a computer records all the data relative to the state of her bodily metabolism and function. Another one at the Internal Revenue Service (did you say, service?) assesses the accuracy and veracity of last year's tax return. And it is darkly rumored that an unknown data bank of unknown location, but government ownership, knows things about her career and private life which she herself has already forgotten.

But it is no insult to her intelligence or education to note that of all these processes she may have hardly a hint of technical comprehension; and certainly she will never need to worry about the maintenance and repair of all the prodigious machines which have become a commanding element of her environment. Unless she or her husband happens to be a scientist or engineer, they probably have less understanding of the components of the whole technological society than do their sons and daughters in high school. This is not only an occasion for irritation and frustration at times, but a cause for concern in the determining of social policy in a democratic state. The Swedish radiation expert, Bo Lindell, says of "society split into one literate and one illiterate subpopulation":

> Problems arise when the majority do not have the basic knowledge of facts and terminology to understand the specialists. The popular participation in determining technological policy in a democratic society is therefore often limited to crude "yes" or "no" decisions based on perceived consequences.[4]

Illustrations abound, drawn from parliamentary decisions in Britain, France, the U.S.A., and Japan, of how some far-reaching policies on both technological expansion and restriction have been approved by legislators who had neither adequate knowledge of technical data nor wisdom to foresee the economic and social consequences of their votes.

The "multiplication of knowledge and the increased specialization of disciplines" has now led to what Warner R. Schilling calls the "mounting sense of impotence on the part of technical-urban man."[5]

BETTER LIVING THROUGH TECHNOLOGY?

How much better is one's life today because of modern technology? That depends largely upon which "one" is meant. Many discussions of this highly pertinent question presuppose as normative the rather affluent cities of Western Europe and America or the wealthy segments of society elsewhere. The pictures drawn of superfluity of improvements, conveniences, and accumulations of consumer goods are not without corresponding reality. Lewis Mumford designates the problem of overabundance by the paradoxical name, "deprivation by surfeit."[6] But such references ignore the large proportion of citizens of these same countries and of the rest of the world whose modest income or dire poverty exclude easy access to the technological cornucopia.

It can be argued that technology is neutral, of ambiguous value and variable detriment to both rich and poor, but in different ways in each case. Changes for better or worse have come quickly when measured on the time scale of centuries, and yet imperceptibly in the consciousness of most people. Predictions of prodigious inventions are often announced sensationally in popular journals, followed in a short time by the invention itself. Soon after being patented the complicated chemical names of antibiotic medicines become familiar in print and conversation. One "miracle drug" follows another to the shelves of pharmacies and even of cut-rate stores. Small black-and-white television screens grow in widths and become even more colorful than reality. Automatic dishwashers, which were a curious luxury not long ago, have become standard kitchen equipment. Adjusting the thermostat—even in time of expensive fuel—is somewhat easier than keeping the coal furnace stoked and banked. In office suites secretaries, who only recently learned to change from manual to electric typewriters, are learning how to attend the intricate machines which "process" words and figures.

These innovations in affluent societies only illustrate how many changes are being introduced, accepted, and adopted. In the whole

11

industry of food production—agriculture, fishing, meat and dairy processing—the effects of scientific technology continue to make today's methods obsolete tomorrow.

Most pervasive and widespread, perhaps, are the new products of the chemical industry. Whether or not many people agree that they enjoy "better living through chemistry," they cannot ignore the extent to which plastics and other synthetics have become substitutes for leather, rubber, wool, cotton, steel, wood, glass, and paper. Chemistry also provides substitutes for food and drink: artificial orange juice, coffee whitener, soybean hamburgers, and artificial ice cream. Vitamins come in pills; synthetic flavoring and aromas challenge the sensory nerves to tell whether they are as pleasing as natural stimuli. Even in a country so productive of wines as Italy, deceivers have been able to fool the wine-loving people with vast quantities of artificial *vino rosso* made without benefit of grapes.

These applications of chemical technology have been displeasing to people of refined taste. The feel of virgin wool in worsted or tweed can hardly be matched by synthetic fabrics (the manufacturers of which also advertise articles made of "virgin vinyl"). Neither can a tabletop of "wood grained" plastic offer the aesthetic satisfaction of a polished walnut or mahogany. And as for tastes and smells—one hardly needs to be a connoisseur or gourmet to know the difference. Despite these negative considerations, the great volume of retail sales of synthetic materials in countries on all continents testifies to the limitless demand and apparent satisfaction of millions of people. With the increase of population and the diminishing supply of natural raw materials—especially of those which cannot be produced domestically in adequate amount at low cost—people would be unable to buy the shoes, clothes, furniture, and certain foods which they desire and can afford. Moreover, it is obvious that for the making of very many articles plastics are not a mere substitute for, but are much superior to, conventional metals, wood, and fiber.

For it is not only the wealthier people of the world whose ways of working, buying, consuming, and relaxing have been generally improved by technology. Those in industrially developed countries who live on the economically defined level of poverty, or below it, nevertheless have available to them a range of possessions about which the truly destitute of the world can only dream: indoor plumbing, electric kitchens and appliances, televisions, and even automobiles. The people of the economically austere German Democratic Republic, for example, can look with envy on the abundance of commodities and luxuries in the other Germany to the West. But they do look on *television sets*, such as the poor of the world can never own. For the German Democratic Republic is economically the most favored of the East European bloc of nations, and Russian shoppers queue up for East German products.

It is not the technological revolution by itself which accounts for the relatively high prosperity and living standard: it is this plus the economic system which has engendered and developed it. That system is capitalism. And it would require a person of strong bias against the facts, or an ignorance of them, to disagree with a statement of the Columbia University philosopher William Barrett:

> We should not forget, on those occasions when we are railing against it, that only through capitalistic organization have we been able in this country in less than a century to raise fifty percent of our people to a standard of living once enjoyed by only one percent.[7]

However accurate the percentages may be, this claim for America can be matched in some other capitalistic countries, but not all. It is only where the capitalist economy has been mated with a ready supply of raw materials, a democratic political structure, public education, and the organizing of trade unions that the benefits of technology have been so widely shared and have resulted in such dramatic improvement in the conditions of living. This general observation may seem to be a boastful statement about the United States. It is not and need not be. "Technical progress is a function of bourgeois money," asserts Jacques Ellul.[8] The economic miracles of Western Europe and Japan since 1948 are the best warrant for its truth.

In the two years following the end of that most destructive of all wars, economists and sociologists were predicting decades of social desolation in the countries which had suffered most from military policies of "scorched earth" and "obliteration bombing." Indeed, the spectacles of unrelieved ruin and rubble in Hamburg, Frankfurt, Coventry, Rotterdam, Nagasaki, and Tokyo seemed to confirm without question the predictions of continued chaos. Germany, they said, would become and remain an agrarian nation; Japan, a pitiable dependent of its American victors. Their formidable prewar industries would never be allowed to arise, it was believed, because the incurably militaristic dispositions of these peoples could never again be permitted to have the means of arms production. So it was said and widely believed.

What the baleful prophets entirely failed to see was the irrepressible vigor of the technological mind. However great the loss of people with scientific imagination and technical skill by wartime death and emigration, those remaining were of sufficient number and vitality to equal and surpass the productivity of previous times of peace. Research and development, required and expedited for the pursuance of total war, had hastened the latest technological revolution. Given those immeasurable resources of scientific knowledge of the survivors, as well as financial aid such as America's Marshall Plan of "enlightened self-interest," the incipient capital funding, and the nearly fanatical hard work of designers, engineers, workers, and managers—given these, the outpouring of productive machinery, building construction, and consumer goods of every description took place within a mere decade. Hong Kong, symbol of technological abundance, quickly became a major outlet for goods from nearby Japan and distant West Germany.

Other European countries, not demolished by the war but exhausted of strength, also made spectacular recoveries and advances in industrial, chemical, electronic, and biological production. American tourists who look for quaint towns and peasant rusticity in Europe are both astonished and disappointed to see that countries of traditional culture and folklore are as far advanced as technological societies with high standards of living. Tourists are even more amazed to see the extent of industrial development in such lands as South Korea, Taiwan, India, Kenya, Nigeria, and several in South America. Likewise, the bloc of socialist countries in East Europe has gone much further in technological productivity and popular distribution than Westerners usually like to think.

All this evidence seems to show that technology based upon experimental science has won a decisive victory over former, and sometimes ancient, techniques of supplying the usable goods and services which people require for an acceptably good life. Is it not, then, quite possible to adopt a sanguine and optimistic attitude toward the values and

14

"blessings" of technology? Thanks to this great combine of productive skill and power, especially in the most industrially developed countries, the Santa Claus bag has been increasingly stuffed by the achievements of scientific researchers, inventors, and manufacturers; and we, with shining eyes and eagerly outstretched hands, have received far more satisfying and pleasurable commodities than the older prophets of utopia imagined—and more than we actually need for a life of material comfort.

Moreover, the effects of technological achievements upon social and political institutions and processes are more important for the mode and meaning of our lives than the quantitative increase of consumer products. Throughout their societies, many countries have now become what Zbigniew Brzezinski called *technetronic.*[9]

There are, in general, three ways of viewing this dominating characteristic of our modern era: uncritical optimism, hypercritical pessimism, and critical optimism. The third is not an inevitable synthesis of the first thesis and its antithesis, however. Each view commends itself for its own reasons.

UNCRITICAL OPTIMISM

Writers of popular utopian literature, from Thomas More and Francis Bacon to B. F. Skinner and Buckminster Fuller have emphasized the techniques and machines by which drudgery, illness, and unhappiness would be mitigated or overcome. Some have shown astonishing prescience, foreseeing submarines, flying machines, and space travel several centuries before science fiction became a literary form and the fiction a reality. Yet, the prophets of only four decades ago who placed a naive faith in a beneficient technocracy were both too modest and too sanguine in their prognostications. A study was made in 1937 by a group of experts under the United States government's auspices to preview developments to be expected in the coming decade; among the fairly significant matters they failed to mention were antibiotics, jet propulsion, radar, and atomic fission! Of course, they also failed to envision the dreadful war, only two years away, which would purchase marvelous advances in technology at the cost of revived barbarism and millions of wasted lives.

The optimist considers only the humanly benign and value-enhancing

15

products of science-based technology: he disregards or minimizes its damaging effects, and wistfully hopes that human avarice, stupidity, and ruthlessness will not corrupt the potential for good. "I'm absolutely convinced," remarked scientist Harrison Brown, "that our science and technology placed in our hands the power to create a world in which everyone has the opportunity of leading a meaningful life, a life divorced from starvation, deprivation and misery." Then, after briefly musing on the countervailing madness of militarism, he concludes, "Nevertheless, we have that power, and perhaps we will come to our senses, mobilize it, and create that kind of world."[10]

What will all people enjoy if "we will come to our senses" and deploy our national budgets and brainpower for technological development? The confident predictions are made, not by the drafters of comic books with their cotton-candy mentalities, but by serious and noted authorities in science and social philosophy.

Thanks to existent genetic and cytological knowledge as well as biomedical techniques, societies of well-born people, virtually free from congenital defects, will be bred. Men and women who "come to their senses" and employ the technical means of contraception, abortion, and rational management of death for those whose lives, for reason of illness, are "meaningless," will lower the rate of population growth to zero. However, hormones and surgical procedures for the transplanting of organs or implanting of artificial devices will extend the healthy lives of those whose lives are "meaningful."

Technology will speed ahead on its present course of removing from personal minds the functions which cybernetic machines can perform. Raising children from infancy to preadolescence, teaching their minds to store quantities of data and to respond to symbolic stimuli, relieving them of the tedium of having to ponder questions and make their own decisions—all these and related effects will be achieved by the widening use of electronic techniques.

Computerized transmitting, storing, and classifying of information will rapidly replace printed means, as has happened to a considerable extent already. The comprehensive new science with the coined name "informatics" will enable technicians to facilitate, and perhaps to regulate, most of the communication between persons which is not spoken and heard face-to-face. But even that—facing one another—will be experienced by two-way television over any distance.

Automation and robots are already at work, and not only in sci-fi films about intergalactic wars. Not without a sense of anxiety, automation expert Thomas B. Sheridan reports that robots are now preferred in certain factories because they are cheaper and more reliable than human workers. They are "quicker, stronger, more precise and more dependable than people,"[11] and they need no lunch breaks, changes of shift, vacations or union organization! As robots take over more and more tasks of manufacturing, human workers will be emancipated from drudgery (it is said) and freed for more "creative" use of time and energy.

Coming under the new modes of effortless production will be food —oil, grains, vegetables, meats, and their artificial substitutes—enough for all in a controlled population.

The social planning required by technological advances will be assumed increasingly by bureaucracies made up of scientifically trained personnel, the prototypes of which are already found abundantly today, seated at thousands of desks, conference tables, and computer panels. Depending upon the place which any nation occupies on the spectrum between democracy and totalitarianism, these bureaucracies will operate within both public and private sectors. Except for taxation and enforcement of laws, the two kinds of bureaucracy will be so influential in determining and directing the patterns of most individual lives that they will seem to be indistinguishable. But the optimistic hope is that a society fully programmed for human well-being and technologically equipped to implement the program will function effectively through an alliance of public and private organizations. Marxist optimists see only the state as the power.

The one major deterrent to all these and similar bounties, as noted by Harrison Brown and many others, is the high cost of militarism and the catastrophic effect upon humanity of a nuclear war. But even here, the optimist can show with confidence that the technological "balance of terror," resting upon the superabundance of weapons of total destructiveness, has kept the hundred or so wars since 1945 within manageable safety. As to the future, confidence can be placed in a just and justifiable rearrangement of the modes of production and distribution, so the minimal needs of poor people everywhere will be met and their self-dependent economic development assured in coming years.

The abundant literature of futurism, or futurology, leaves nothing for the most fertile imagination to envision about the technological society. Some projections are written to shock, some to satirize, and some to whet the collective appetite for a better tomorrow.

HYPERCRITICAL PESSIMISM

According to a fictitious lawgiver named Murphy, if things can go wrong, they will. This is how the course of scientific technology is seen by many contemporary observers and prophets. They are not ready to move to Lalibela, nor take up spinning, weaving, and tailoring to make their own clothes. But the manifest conveniences and benefits resulting from three centuries of technical progress are now overshadowed by the dark clouds of imminent chaos and doom. Too much of any good thing is bad.

If the expressive arts are the antennae of culture, they began sounding the alarm signals years ago. Hermann Hesse's man of fiction aimed his rifle at private motor cars as he would at invading tanks. Franz Kafka's nemesis was the faceless bureaucracy of the modern state, but for George Orwell the big brotherly face was only too visible. Charlie Chaplin was the "little man" of the world who was crushed by the machines of modern times. And Picasso's canvas showed men and horses being torn and shattered by military steel and fearful concussion at Guernica. Painting, sculpture, poetry, and the theater have said concisely what writers and preachers have argued in prolix discussions: technology is a mixed good at best; a demonic threat at worst.

Strong feeling makes vivid rhetoric come easily. "It is my conviction that the technological society is the dragon which needs to be killed," exclaimed Brazilian philosopher, Rubem Alves. Science and technology were once tools for creativity and instruments of life, he said. Now, because they have forfeited their freedom to impersonal powers of political, economic, and military oppression, "they are the dragon's poisonous sting."[12] It seems to make little difference which kind of political system employs and exploits the machines, processes, and myths of technology. All are oppressive, robbing the masses of people

18

of their integrity, dignity, or livelihood. The totalitarian Communist state uses technology for building up the power of the few in the name of all. The totalitarian Fascist state does the same, but in the name of the few. The semisocialistic and capitalistic democracies are at the mercy of gigantic corporations, which disregard human values and crush people simply because they, as corporate entities serving the few, are enslaved by the technological ideology of unlimited production and expansion.

Those who speak for particular segments of the citizenry express the same angry complaint. In a racially and ethnically mixed society technological power is in the hands of whites, and that means financial and political power as well. Voices of the feminist revolution charge indisputably that these powers are held and guarded by males.

One who most thoroughly and gloomily analyzes the problem is the Frenchman, Jacques Ellul. He is a social scientist, lawyer, Protestant theologian, and prolific writer. For him, technology and technique are one, and the meaning is the *"totality of methods rationally arrived at and having absolute efficiency* in *every* field of human activity."[13] Capitalism and Marxism alike share in adulation of technique. "In our time," he wrote in 1953, "everything that is not technique is being eliminated."[14] The essential, and not merely traditional, human qualities of freedom, initiative, individuality, personal caring, and hope are being smothered by endemic technique; they are replaced by submissiveness, docility, conformity, self-centered anxiety, and cynicism.

In the industrial countries of Europe and the Americas this irreversible displacement of human qualities has been in process for nearly two centuries, much accelerated in the present one. In the recently decolonized nations of Africa and Asia, the same is happening within only two decades. The yearning of civil leaders in developing countries for more extensive and more efficient technology is, according to this view, a death wish. It has already led to a melancholy array of petty dictatorships, anarchy, metastatized urban slums, and hopelessly disrupted economies. This happens when the exercise of rationality and efficiency is controlled by an oligarchy which lusts after technical means for securing its own gratification. Where technology is well established, as in Europe and the Americas, and governments are rather stable, the consequences of the system are less dramatic and traumatic: just the draining of human beings of their proper humanity.

In Ellul's concept, technique is not a neutral instrument by which good leaders bring forth good societies and evil leaders corrupt ones. In his pessimistic way he shows that the good are helpless to prevent the social and human debilitation which is the irrepressible effect of technology. He takes the same dark view of urban life, which is inherently corrupting, because cities are the product of technology and not merely its context.

Westward across the Atlantic, Lewis Mumford has pondered for fifty years the malaise of modern technological culture, its arts, institutions, cities, fractured hopes, and disasters. He is not a doctrinaire technophobe, revolting against modern trends because of romanticism about nature or nostalgia for past history. His vigorous attack on "megatechnics" and "megamachines," as he calls them, is fortified by an intimate and comprehensive knowledge of the history of cultures and science; it is motivated by a passion for the enhancement of the qualities of humanity which are held in highest esteem by persons of culture in every high civilization.

Three quotations from the huge treasury of his writing give the point of his anguished criticism:

> How long . . . can the physical structure of an advanced technology hold together when all its human foundations are crumbling away? All this has happened so suddenly that many people are hardly aware that it has happened at all; yet during the last generation the very bottom has dropped out of our life; the human institutions and moral convictions that have taken thousands of years to achieve even a minimal efficacy have disappeared before our eyes: so completely that the next generation will scarcely believe they ever existed.[15]

> An age like our own, whose subjectivity trusts only one channel, that through science and technology, is ill-prepared to face the stark realities of life. Even those who still cling to the ancient heritage of religion and art, rich and nourishing though that still is, have become so acclimated to the dehumanized assumptions of technology that only a scattering of faithful souls have dared to challenge even its grossest perversions.[16]

> For who can doubt that destructions and massacres, the environmental depletions and the human degradations that have become prevalent during the last half century have been in direct propor-

tion to the dynamism, power, speed, and instantaneous control that megatechnics has promoted?[17]

Where Ellul finds the fatal fault in the idolizing of rationality and efficiency, Mumford discerns it in the paradigm of the machine. The faults are not identical, but related; and they stem from a common source. The source is the rationalism of René Descartes and his divorce of one's thinking mind from all perceived objects, including other persons. His epoch-making *Discourse on the Method* in the early seventeenth century gave primacy to the thinking mind over its objects. It also inspired European philosophers and scientists to share his certitude that a mechanistic explanation of the world could be their legitimate and feasible goal. For nearly two hundred years thereafter, the model for nature, for each organism, for each human being, was that of a machine. When theorists after Darwin and Einstein abandoned the mechanistic notion of the structure of organisms and of inanimate composites, the belief persisted among the applicators and practitioners of techniques that the machine, logically constructed and efficiently operating, was still the prime model not only for physics and physiology but for human society as well. What were missing from Descartes's view and also from an understanding of the modern megamachine, notes Mumford, were "history, symbolic culture, mind—in other words, the totality of human experience *not simply as known but as lived.*"[18] The technology which prevails today is affirmed, supported, and advanced by those who still cannot recognize the superiority of human values over mathematical and mechanical forms. Until that recognition becomes widespread and effectual, the dehumanizing apparatus of technology will expand and thrive without hindrance.

Everyone knows the prodigious fecundity of technological manufacturing and provision of effectual systems of social services, communication, and control. Many of these are of inestimable value; they would be relinquished most reluctantly. But they belong to the megamachine which produces not only things which are manifestly good for man's health and comfort but also those which thrust him downward and backward from the cultural ascent. "The sorcerer's gift of fire in a dark cave has brought us more than a simple kingdom," warns Loren Eisely, "Like so many magical gifts, it has conjured up that which cannot be subdued but henceforth demands unceasing attention lest it destroy us."[19]

CRITICAL OPTIMISM

The difference between uncritical and critical optimism in assessing technology as a total system is that the former has full trust in its salutary effect upon human living while the latter, in a mood of cautious skepticism, imposes qualifying questions. The pessimist, as we have seen, is convinced that the direction of humanity under technological control is hopelessly pejorative.

Psychologist Erich Fromm saw the inherent dangers in a regnant technology, but he reserved both approbation and condemnation until it can be determined whether the essentials of human morality can be preserved within a society so dominated. This position provokes two observations. One is that Fromm, or other citizens acting in concert, could do little to change the spread of technology. The other is that people's concepts of the essentials of morality are neither uniform nor universal. Yet Fromm thought that we know "the goals common to all humanist philosophical and religious systems of the West and East," and these are the criteria for judging the degree to which a society of culture approximates them. They stem from a basic sense of awe before the reality of life (Albert Schweitzer's reverence for life). They include: overcoming greed, loving one's neighbor, striving to know what is true.

> Any real hope for victory over the dehumanized society of the megamachine and for the building up of a humanist industrial society rests upon the condition that the values of the tradition are brought to life, and that a society emerges in which love and integrity are possible.[20]

In contrast to Ellul and Mumford, Fromm wrote that he saw "a somewhat greater possibility of restoring the social system to man's control" according to such moral criteria.

When one considers the technological society for what it is—the mountainous organizations of research, manufacture, and distribution, with occupations for millions of people and investments of trillions of dollars, all related in many ways to the gargantuan structures of government—it may seem naive and sentimental to apply to them standards of human respect, restraint, and love. But Fromm was most serious in proposing the primacy of such values to guide persons who bear responsibility for these massive enterprises which shape society and affect human lives. This is the proper, if often futile, vocation of the philosopher: advising the merchant and politician.

In *Technological Man* Victor C. Ferkiss shows neither enthusiasm nor dread for what is rapidly occurring in America to bring almost everything under technological influence. While he shares Fromm's hopefulness, his conditions and questions are different. First, he agrees that the touchstone of technology is its positive effect on morality. But in contrast to Fromm—and even more, to any Christian moralists—Ferkiss is quite agnostic concerning the definition of moral values. Indeed, he writes, "Technological man, by definition, will be possessed of the world view of science and technology, which will themselves provide a standard of value for future civilization."[21] As he perceives these autogenerated values, they include recognition of three principles: man's continuity with nature, the interconnectedness of all phenomena in the process of becoming, and the immanent this-worldly nature of reality. What at first reading he seems to say is that science and technology will impose scientific materialism on human society, subjecting humanity to these materialist masters. But this is not intended. For the second condition posed by Ferkiss is that the one who can be designated technological man will be in control of technology, even as he is "in control of his own development within the context of a meaningful philosophy of the role of technology in human evolution."[22] Who is this person? Where is he? Ferkiss reiterates his belief that this competent, controlling kind of person can hardly be said to exist as yet. Americans still conform to the types of "the economic man of industrial society or the liberal democratic man of the bourgeois political order."[23] But his hope is in the imminent coming of *homo technologicus*.

The ideas of Fromm and Ferkiss are representative of two kinds of critical optimism, according to which the further development of technology can be evaluated and affirmed. Their views could be amplified by discussion of dozens of books and conference reports on the subject, most of which seem to favor critical optimism. And in most cases the critical questions are not the ones which first occur to some molders and manipulators of technology. What is the cost benefit? What will it do for business? What value does it have for military readiness? What are the second and third order impacts upon social institutions and communities? These are technical questions dealt with by the newly emerging social science called Technology Assessment. It is practiced especially by consultants to governments and business corporations. Ironically, it is itself a sophisticated form of technology. It is "the latest in a long line of techniques which purport to extend the rigors of scientific method from the physical and biological sciences to the economic, political and social ones," writes British assessor Michael Gibbons.[24] He opposes a popular intention that such programs of analysis should be as nearly "value-free" as possible—the sterile myth of objectivity and total detachment. In addition to the admittedly important questions of cost effectiveness and social impact of technological innovations (like jet travel, credit cards, cable television, nuclear power plants) we must ask: By what moral insights and norms do we conceive human good? Who is responsible for protecting children and youth from the seductiveness of consumerism? What effect will a technique have upon the social and economic conditions of ethnic and racial minorities?— and such other *human* questions which now lead to some theological concerns about technology.

WHY IS TECHNOLOGY A MATTER FOR THEOLOGY?

Obviously one need not embrace a religious faith, Christian or another, to share some of the hopes and sensitivities which religion conveys to its adherents. People who are condescendingly referred to as secularists often exceed individual Christians in manifesting the Christians' specified virtues. Conversely, it should be acknowledged that theological concerns are not limited to narrowly religious or moral attitudes and practices. The whole phenomenon of science-based technology is very much a subject for theological interpretation, criticism, and influence. This has been graphically demonstrated by the serious attention paid to technological matters by the World Council of Churches during the past decade.

One of the most pressing concerns of the churches is to measure the effects of technological expansion upon the poor, excluded, and oppressed people of two-thirds of the world. Of course, they have no copyright on this sense of responsibility. Especially in the United Nations circles, these people are gaining a hearing for their needs and just aspirations. The 1979 conference in Vienna on Science and Technology for Development provided a global rostrum. And the governments of many more affluent nations, and private associations within them, are devoting much effort and money to programs of technical assistance. It is, therefore, a conspicuous lack in secular writing on science and technology when authors, without justifying the omission, say nothing about equity and justice for the disadvantaged and economically repressed majority of the world's population. They write as though only their own country, or their own social stratum were important. Such provincialism is unacceptable in this time of global interdependence.

For Christians, the universality of human interdependence is an article of faith. It springs from belief in the undelineated love of the Creator for every human being. The Bible teaches that God is perennially on the side of the poor and dispossessed, whom those who are well-off have a moral obligation to help. The global spread, cultural diversity, and universal community of the Christian Church—despite its many deficiencies—is a clear sign of this faith. A World Council of Churches report explains it well:

> The God of the prophets and Jesus Christ allies and identifies Himself with those who are poor and marginal in society. Hence we regard the obligation to promote a just distribution of the world's resources as a basic principle in a Christian political ethics. Social justice should therefore be one of the main criteria for planning technological development in the future society. Our task as Christians should be to discover how the resources of modern technology can be used to bridge the existing gaps between classes, people and nations.[25]

These words are rhetoric, to be sure. But the churches are actually doing far more today to put the words into effective action than is generally known.

Christianity teaches not only care for all persons but also an expectation that sudden changes in personal and social situations will be wrought by the acts of avaricious people. The reaping of a whirlwind comes in surprising ways after the sowing of earlier winds of greed and hostility. Put another way, there is no dependable course of his-

25

tory: the evil and good uses of human freedom upset any ideas of fatalism or inevitable progress. Thus writers on technology before 1975 show their insensitivity to the theological insight of historical unpredictability. None seems to have expected any disruption of technology's progress by the sudden withdrawal of crude oil from the low-cost markets of the world. If there is any requisite of technology it is energy. Here is a paradox: industrial technology lives upon irreplaceable fossil fuels, but the more technology thrives upon such resources, the more it threatens its own future development. Consider, then, how the tidy theories (optimistic or pessimistic) about technology go into a nose dive when oil is suddenly a limited commodity. In a perspective drawn from the Bible, the one certainty about historical events is their uncertainty.

Yet, God's purposes in human history are certain, if particular sequences of events are not. To assert that God, the Creator, has intentions and plans for the human race, and for the communities and persons within it, is not a scientifically warranted statement in the accepted sense. But it is as certain and fundamental to the Christian understanding as a law of thermodynamics is to physics. That purpose is called "salvation," but it includes more than the conventional meaning of an individual human's "going to heaven." Salvation is also temporal and terrestrial; it is corporate, communal, and social as well as personal. It is as historically real and personal as the man Jesus Christ of Nazareth, in whom God has come to effect reconciliation and new life.

Such thinking might be dismissed as so much pious but empty talk. No doubt it amounts only to that for many nominal Christians, or for those who are still uninformed about the cognitive content of the faith —which is theology. But the doctrine of God's purpose and action in history means that he allows all the tragedies and regressions which sinful humans bring upon themselves by the exercise of their freedom; and he always holds forth the way, the power, and the hope of fulfillment. The rise and flourishing of science and technology have a place in that plan because of their powerful effect upon the way millions of people live. But, like every other historical movement, institution, or system of activity in human relations, they are subject to the judgment of divine goodness. Or better, the men and women who wield the powers of technology—such as communications media, transportation, commerce, and education—are accountable to that judgment for the human effects of their work.

Those powers not only tempt people who control them to use them for the self-serving ends of satisfying inordinate greed at the expense of other person's suffering; they also keep stimulating the appetites of passive consumers to acquire more and more products of superfluous utility or dubious intrinsic value. When technology exceeds its warranted purpose of enabling people to satisfy their basic needs and moderate wants, it becomes more and more the tyrannous master of human behavior instead of the supporting servant. After softening the *hard* materialism of those who have too little for a good life, the technological economy inflates the *soft* materialism of those who have too much and always desire more.

This abuse of the means of supporting human life can become idolatry in a more than figurative sense. Allegiance to God and his revealed will is transferred to the mechanical and cybernetic deity "from whom all blessings flow." The disposition to practice idolatry, to worship the material creature rather than the spiritual Creator, is ancient and still endemic. Modern technology, while manifestly beneficient in countless ways, still sets before humanity a much greater temptation to enslaving idolatry than any little idols carved of wood or stone. And slavery of mind, spirit, and even of body is the correlative of idolatry. As Jacques Ellul discerns this destructive process:

> The individual who lives in the technical milieu knows very well that there is nothing spiritual anywhere. But man cannot live without the sacred. He therefore transfers his sense of the sacred to the very thing which has destroyed its former object; to technique itself.[26]

So an earthly host of technolatrists sing their Doxology to the god which is fashioned by their own ingenuity and divinized by their misplaced credulity.

The primary concern of Christian faith is not defensive, but affirmative: not to defend the holiness of the one God against detractors, but to affirm and enhance the lives of "all creatures here below," especially those who as humans bear the stamp of his image.

"Technology is a human achievement," concludes ethicist Roger L. Shinn, "Hence, it is a human responsibility. It is for mankind to direct technology, not to be victimized by it. In the course of events, technology has come to remind mankind of what is not a human achievement, but a divine gift: life, this earth, the stirrings of the spirit that makes this human race discontent with what is."[27]

NOTES

1. Victor C. Ferkiss, *Technological Man* (New York: New American Library, 1969), p. 28.

2. Lewis Mumford, *The Pentagon of Power* (New York: Harcourt Brace Jovanovich, 1970), p. 127.

3. Amilcar O. Herrera, "Science, Technology and Society in Latin America," *Anticipation* (Geneva: World Council of Churches), 17 (May 1974): 46.

4. Bo Lindell, "Ethical and Social Issues in Risk Management," *Faith and Science in an Unjust World,* vol. 1 (Philadelphia: Fortress Press, 1980), p. 126.

5. Warner R. Schilling, "Technology and International Relations," *International Encyclopedia of the Social Sciences,* vol. 15 (New York: Macmillan, 1968), p. 596.

6. Mumford, *Pentagon of Power,* p. 127.

7. William Barrett, *The Illusion of Technique* (New York: Anchor/Doubleday, 1978), p. 206.

8. Jacques Ellul, *The Technological Society,* trans. John Wilkinson (New York: Alfred Knopf, 1964), p. 54.

9. Zbigniew Brzezinski, "America in the Technetronic Society," *Encounter,* 30, no. 1 (January 1968): 19.

10. Harrison Brown, "Technology and Where We Are," *Technology, Human Values and Leisure,* ed. Max Kaplan and Phillip Bosserman (Nashville, Tenn.: Abingdon Press, 1971), p. 67.

11. Thomas B. Sheridan, "Computer Control and Human Alienation," *Faith and Science,* vol. 1, p. 294.

12. Rubem Alves, "Faith and Ethics in a Technological Society," Address to Science Students' Conference, Wellesley College, Wellesley, Mass., July 1979. See his serious satire, "On the Eating Habits of Science," *Faith and Science,* vol. 1, pp. 41–43.

13. Ellul, *Technological Society,* p. xxv. Ellul's italics.

14. Ibid., p. 84.

15. Mumford, *Pentagon of Power,* p. 432.

16. Ibid., p. 417.

17. Ibid., p. 349.

18. Ibid., p. 91. Mumford's italics.

19. Loren Eisely, *The Unexpected Universe* (New York: Harcourt Brace Jovanovich, 1969), p. 99.

20. Erich Fromm, *The Revolution of Hope* (New York: Harper and Row, 1968), p. 89.

21. Ferkiss, *Technological Man,* p. 203.

22. Ibid., p. 202.

23. Ibid., p. 201.

24. Michael Gibbons, "Technology Assessment: Objectivity or Utopia?" *Technology as Institutionally Related to Human Values,* ed. Philip C. Ritterbush (Washington: Acropolis Books, 1974), p. 59.

25. "The Technological Future of the Industrialized Nations and the Quality of Life," *Anticipation,* 15 (December 1973): 7.

26. Ellul, *Technological Society,* p. 143.

27. Roger L. Shinn, "The Impact of Science and Technology on the Theological Understanding of Social Justice," *Anticipation,* 17 (May 1974): 59.

2 | Science and Faith: Their Comparability and Compatibility

How can we understand what and who we are? How can we know the environment we exist in, the myriad phenomena of nature, of earth and the cosmos? Both religion and science have evolved in the course of human effort to answer these same primordial questions.

To say that science asks "how?" and religion asks "why?" is a misleading and erroneous simplification of their distinctiveness.

To observe that science is the realm of reason and religion the attitude of nonreasoning belief is not only to distort reality but to deceive and fortify prejudices against one or the other.

To claim that scientists know something only by observation, measurement, mathematics, and experimental control, while religionists (dreadful word!) know only by divine revelation or intuition is another popular but erroneous distinction. But to assert, as some do, that there are no fundamental differences between science and religion is to disregard the critical perception of the evidence.

How, then, can we explain the well-attested religious affirmations of certain great scientists and many who are highly respected, or the scientific sophistication of theologians and religious thinkers?[1] Large quantities of serious literature combine with familiar arguments about science and faith to assure us of one conviction: namely, that something of primal importance for human existence is at stake in the kinds of answers given to the basic "how?" and "why?" questions about ourselves and the natural world. Sooner or later, both scientific and religious inquiries lead to matters of ultimate concern for all persons.[2]

In the complexity of present civilization the concern for ultimacy is not limited to scientific or religious thought. Either domain can be linked to others which then, in their intercourse, raise up the most

31

urgent issues of human knowledge, well-being, survival, and destiny. Thus we could explore the mutual relations of science and economics, economics and religion, religion and politics, politics and science, science and humanities, humanities and religion, all of which meet like nerve endings. Each synapse provides a different and distinct way of grappling with ultimate issues.

Two uncertainties make the comparisons between science and religion (or faith) difficult to specify. One is the lack of consistency in the category known as religion; the second is the difficulty of designating a person who fully represents religion (or faith). All efforts to give to religion a unified definition which has a really practical use seem doomed to failure. And a clear and usable distinction between a scientist and a religionist is also beyond our reach. To put a Buddhist philosopher, a Brahmin priest, and a Catholic theologian on one side of the table, across from an astronomer, a biochemist, and a high-energy physicist, whose religious views are not specified, would seem to meet the requirements of a good dialogue on science and faith. Such artificiality of pairing is of the same spurious character, however, as much vulgarized talk of science and religion. The dialogue can have meaning only if members of each side share the same, or similar, presuppositions: those of a recognized religious type on one side, those of a certain philosophy of science or common discipline on the other.

Who, for the purpose of this present discussion, should sit on the side of the table first mentioned? Not adherents of any or all religions, but those committed to the biblically-based faith of monotheistic Judaism and Christianity. And for certain parts of the discussion, Christians would need to speak for themselves apart from Judaism. Those would be at such times as affirmations are made about God's self-disclosure in Jesus Christ. It may happen that on certain convictions not only Jews and Christians but people of other Asiatic or Occidental faiths could concur. Such might be a shared belief in a transcendent or divine evaluation of human life, the reality of spirit, and the conditions for peace.

No invidious judgment on religions other than Christianity and Judaism is intended by this suggestion. Nor is it implied that insights found in, say, Islam or Buddhism lack validity and truth or appropriateness to the dialogue with scientists. But religions are not simply aggregates of beliefs, insights, and doctrines. They are social communities with distinctive historical traditions, cultic patterns, moral constraints, and (usually) publicly recognized institutions. The name "religion" can, like a fog, cover all aspects of religions but also conceal what is most important about each.

WHY BOTHER?

Now ask those people whose informed belief and sincere faith qualify them to represent a biblically-based monotheism, "Why are you concerned at all about modern science?" What factors not only incline one, but require one, to reflect upon the presuppositions, claims, and inadequacies of both science and faith?

One factor is curiosity. The human mind compels itself to inquire, to learn, and to know (unless there be mental retardation or such preoccupation with bare subsistence that critical thought is numbed). Knowledge for its own sake is the sufficient warrant for philosophy and "pure" science. With the advent and expansion of mass literacy and education in many countries, the access to scientific knowledge about human beings, their environment and world has suddenly been opened. People of faith are as much attracted to popularized presentations of scientific achievements and to the more demanding literature as are those who profess no faith. While intellectual curiosity is insatiable, so the amount of exciting information made available is seemingly inexhaustible.

Excitement may be less an inducement to seeking scientific knowledge than anxiety, however. There are several good reasons to be anxious.

Anxiety about defending the religious faith is more prevalent among Christians than Jews. Surely it was not confidence about possessing the truth, but anxiety about preserving their claim to truth and to institutional power, which once led the churches to suppress and even destroy philosophers and scientists. Romans today buy their vegetables, meat, and flowers around the statue of Giordano Bruno, who was burned in the Campo dei Fiori in 1600, hardly aware, we can guess, that the bronze is also a monument to the paranoid worry of dogmatic ecclesiastics. And Roman mail is handled in the building where anxious

Dominicans, named for the Galilean who said "Be not anxious," sealed the mouth and mind of Galileo Galilei.

Evocation of the case of Galileo has become a convenient cliché in present polemics against religion and church by the apologists for untrammeled scientific research. No church today has the inclination, much less the will, to excommunicate astrophysicists nor the power to burn scientific materialists in public places. Pope John Paul II, indeed, has called for the church's belated acknowledgment of the greatness of Galileo and of the misjudgment by the church. Speaking to scientists in November 1979, he said: "The collaboration between religion and modern science is to the advantage of both, without in any way violating their respective autonomy."[3] In spite of this changed attitude, deep anxiety remains in the minds of those who feel uneasy over reports that science, like the spring waters under St. Peter's basilica, is threatening to weaken the foundations of faith. This differs from the attacks of robust, aggressive, militant atheists of recent centuries, whose weapons were logic, ridicule, satire, or crude propaganda and the rhetoric of despair. The gentle, effectual influences of atheism, purported to be validated by scientific method, work subtly, often unintentionally, upon the thinking of students and others who hold science in awe. Not by attack, but by unconcerned neglect and elimination of transcendent or metaphysical realities, do scientists, technicians, and teachers of science convey the idea and spread the conviction that the God-hypothesis of Christian faith and other monotheisms has no validity. If empirical, measurable evidence is necessary for the demonstration of a reality, how can the biblical God be seen or quantified? If the truth of an hypothesis or statement depends upon its verifiability or demonstration of its falsity, who is able to provide indisputable evidence for rational minds that "God" is truly God? These challenges of faith are well known to any sophomore student of science or philosophy. They are not frivolous sophistries, though. They put Christian and other theistic thinkers on guard against both the frontal attacks of atheism and the seductive feints of impersonal deism or bland pantheism. Remove the creative, personal God and the whole structure of faith and church collapses.

A second cause for anxiety arises over concern for the meaning, happiness, and security of life for all people. All religions in varying ways have a bearing on the values of living. Biblical monotheism, more than others, gives highest place to love, mercy, compassion, justice, individual dignity, community, and hope in and beyond history. It claims that these universal values are derived from the divine Creator's eternal will and—despite the contrary forces of evil and sin—are sustained by divine energies at work in personal and communal experience.

Without doubt, a religiously agnostic but humanistic scientist can share respect for and belief in some of these religious values, especially those observable in human behavior. Regardless of motivation or explanation, there is a wide range of moral actions wherein religious and humanistic sensitivities coincide. A person perishing of thirst is not likely to demand a reason why someone offers a cup of cold water—whether in the name of Jesus or of human decency. And the powerful struggles for racial liberation and equity in Africa and the United States have shown how the strong compulsions of religious faith converge with ideology and political commitment and unite in causing the same action for justice and freedom.

Why, then, the anxiety about science? Even though the myth of science as being "pure" and "value free" has been decisively discredited, it is not self-evident to everyone why science is a worrisome factor for people of faith. There are reasons enough: four large ones.

Firstly, what are the scientific world view and technological growth doing to the conception of human value and individual identity? It has been a long Sisyphus-like struggle to ascend the hill of human dignity for all persons. The history of slavery, serfdom, torture, infanticide, and genocide has not, unhappily, come to an end. But it has been mitigated since the eighteenth century by movements of democracy, human rights, and massive compassion, all of which spring from a conviction about the intrinsic worth of each person. The ideas that primitive peoples are less than human, that "Jews, Turks, and infidels" are damned, that slaves are (by the U.S. Supreme Court 1857 decision on Dred Scott) not persons, that Jews and gypsies are unworthy of life—these have poisoned the collective human conscience for two millennia. They have been only partially revised in two centuries, during the advent of modern science.

Now comes the threat of another kind, a scientific kind. It is not

35

primarily the false theory of genetics, that some races are superior to others, so that the "others" are worthless. It is the concept of "the naked ape," or the physicochemical organism, or the particular complex of tissues which can be manipulated and "programmed" at will, or the genetically determined package of flesh which is kin to the termite and ant. On the graph of the market report of human value, these attractive ideas of scientific materialism and psychological behaviorism represent a downward trend. Often proposed and commended by people of genial personality, they point toward ultimate horrors at the nadir of the graph: biological mechanization, political regimentation, moral debasement.

The personal reaction, secondly, to scientific cosmology may bring about a similar sense of human unworth. If Copernicus and Galileo "dethroned" humans and the planet earth from their assumed eminence in the universe, Darwin, Freud, Lorenz, and Skinner have—in the opinion of many—consigned humans to a special corner of the planetary zoo. Sober speculations about the possibility, or probability, or even certainty of intelligent life on planets of other galaxies only intensify the sense of cosmic shock. What is man? Nothing!

Informed thinkers of Jewish and Christian religious persuasions have not been baffled or silenced by the scientific assaults on a belief in the anthropocentric universe. Indeed, the findings and theories of astronomy and cosmology have been largely assimilated by Christian theologians; and Freudian insights are used by pastoral counselors in helping people understand and overcome their psychic problems. There is no inevitable reason for people to deduce wholly pessimistic ideas about humanity from the findings and theories about man's littleness in the cosmos and his many affinities to animal life. Moreover, as Norbert Wiener writes of computer science, the offense of comparing man to ape has been exceeded in our time by the sober comparison to a machine. Theory moves to reality as robots are being constructed.[4] Still, these theories do inspire negative conclusions and, in consequence, morose attitudes toward life.

The ecological corruption resulting from uncontrolled growth of science-based technology is a third cause to worry about the human future. The religions derived from the Bible regard nature as an amazing, God-created home for man. It is a seemingly limitless treasure house of necessities for life, wherein the glory of God is reflected in the history of the race. This faith has often been distorted by the spoilers and exploiters of land and sea. In ancient times, the famed cedars of Lebanon and the wooded groves of Hellas were sacrificed to the maritime fleets for commerce and warfare. Arable land was turned into desert, and the herds of grazing animals, fur- and ivory-bearing fauna were slaughtered with exultancy rather than remorse. But who does not know that these ancient assaults upon the natural environment were as nothing compared to the daily outrages of the present? "We are creatures utterly dependent upon a delicate planetary environment— a thin crust of soil and a fragile layer of atmosphere," writes William Barrett, "We are still cosmic animals haunted by some imagination of our place in the scheme of things."[5] This is indeed a crisis situation in which the men and women of faith discover that their compelling religious belief in the obligation of stewardship of God's creation coincides with the elemental drive for survival felt by all sorts of reflective persons. Scientists and nonscientists, believers and agnostics, can with equal vigor work for the prevention of this dreaded ecological catastrophe often predicted.

Debasement of life's value, a sense of cosmic estrangement, and fretful fear of the spoliation of planet earth should suffice to arouse feelings of deep anxiety. But they reach a climax in one more implication of certain scientific theory and technology. This is the pervasive despair felt by those who meditate on the imminent apocalypse of atomic warfare and the ultimate annihilation of the cosmic order because of the entropy of energy and the exploding forces of the galaxies. The nuclear cataclysm is perhaps too near a possibility to contemplate coolly; and the cosmic ending is, in theory, light-years away from our time. Whether near or far, however, they press down upon some sensitive minds the dank gray mood of futility and despair. Not only may the *New* World not be "Brave" but, more likely, this *Old* World will be fading in its congeniality for happy life. Bertrand Russell sounded this thematic note many years before the near and far catastrophes became credible realities. In 1929 he wrote eloquent words often cited:

> That man is the product of causes which had no prevision of the end they were achieving; that his origin, his growth, his hopes and fears, his loves and beliefs, are but the outcome of accidental collo-

cations of atoms . . . all these things, if not quite beyond dispute, are yet so nearly certain that no philosophy which rejects them can hope to stand. Only within the scaffolding of these truths, only on the firm foundation of unyielding despair, can the soul's habitation henceforth be safely built.[6]

Does contemporary science have any bearing upon personal and social ethics? This question clearly receives an affirmative reply and is another main reason why reflective persons of religious faith must come to terms with science. Far from being value-free, science has been exerting increasing influence upon the capacity of persons, institutions, and societies to clarify ethical criteria. This means much more than the fact that science and technology are presenting new and difficult kinds of moral problems, which may or may not be resolved according to traditional rules or by conditioned intuitions. The ethical situation itself, and the shaping of attitudes, have been changed by science.

Whereas religion has long been the custodian, bearer, teacher, and judge of morality, claiming divine sanction for its counsels, some regnant forms of scientific philosophy have ostensibly ousted that authority and wrested the mace of rectitude for themselves. Of first importance, of course, is the view now advanced by many that a person's moral behavior is neither beholden to a divine will nor relevant to one's eternal destiny—since both the divinity and the eternity are dismissed as unknowable or denied as incredible.

Geneticist Francis Crick has no doubt of this change in the moral situation. Writing in response to Lord C. P. Snow, he asserts:

The old, or literary culture, which was based originally on Christian values, is clearly dying, whereas the new culture, the scientific one, based on scientific values, is still in an early stage of development, although it is growing with great rapidity.[7]

The burgeoning since 1970 of studies in medical ethics is a clear example of the new dimension of problems created by such branches of science as endocrinology, pharmacology, oncology, and medical engineering. Most acute among the issues in which religious moralists have strong interest are the organ transplant procedures, resuscitation and artificial prolongation of life by heroic means, and the allocation of scarce or costly medical resources. These beg for yet deeper questions to be clarified: What is health? Who is (becomes or ceases to be) a person? What is death?

Many of the newer problems of attitude and action are in the area of sex, marriage, and reproduction. Not only has the divine judgment against adultery been questioned but the social consequences of pregnancy, illegitimacy, and divorce have been mitigated. The more conservative churches—Catholic, Orthodox, and Protestant alike—are waging a defense of diminishing success against these science-related assaults upon traditional morality. By the same technologies of reproductive control, many women are being emancipated from the role of mother and homemaker, with consequent changes in the moral climate of society. One such change, for example, is the heightening of opportunities for women in employment and public affairs.

Another moral attitude which has been affected by science is the one which is often thought to be the particular province of biblical religion, namely, altruistic love. Loving the other, or neighbor, is the hallmark and epitome of religious ethical teaching. Yet, it is now being claimed by sociobiologists that altruistic love is mainly determined by genetic structures; and further, that it can be adequately induced or inhibited by electrical or chemical determinants applied to the brain.[8]

The alliances of much science and technology with powers of finance, politics, business interests, exploitative commerce, and militarism constitute a formidable array of new and spreading moral issues. For one thing, the sheer mass and energy of these alliances in developed countries have the effect of overwhelming and neutralizing the moral protests of individuals and groups which perceive dangers in such complicity. Further, it is these powerful economic and political interests, both the patrons and exploiters of scientific programs, that are able to determine national priorities of policy. What these policies may be—for example, less technical aid to certain African countries, more military sales to others, controls on certain kinds of experimentation and drugs—are the concern of all responsible citizens, but they are particularly high on the working agenda of church agencies and religiously motivated organizations. Is it conceivable that scientific associations could recognize the value of sharing alliances of information and counsel with some competent religious agencies? There is probably more reason for common cause than is generally thought. An adversary relation between religion and science should never be presupposed, though such may prove to be the unavoidable case.

ARE THEY BEYOND COMPARE?

Science and faith are disparate but not absolutely so. This means that despite their distinct difference they are comparable rather than incomparable. To compare them and show the possible varieties of their relationship is not only a reasonable and pleasant possibility, as one might compare rugby football with volleyball; it is a matter of seriousness about how we grasp, analyze, and try to cope with issues of major, and even ultimate, significance for human existence.

COMPARABLE IN STRUCTURE

Are they comparable in structure as well as in the seriousness of their undertakings? Wang Hsien-Chih of Taiwan has proposed four constituent aspects of science and faith which, though differing immensely, make comparison possible.[9]

Each has a characteristic methodology. This would include for most sciences such steps as fact gathering, measuring, analyzing, experimenting under controlled conditions, repeating experiments, and theorizing —all done according to what Robert K. Merton calls "disinterestedness and organized skepticism."[10] The method of faith and its intellectual handmaid, theology, comprises fact gathering from all kinds of human experience, reflecting on wisdom and insights of scripture and church tradition, philosophical criticism, prayer and illumination, application to actions of service, mission, ethics, and worship.

There is enough congruity between methods used in scientific and theological investigation to warrant the idea that theology itself is a "scientific" discipline. Due to the usage and connotation of the word *Wissenschaft* (literally, condition of knowing), Germans can easily and accurately designate theology as a science: a mode of knowing and of employing knowledge of God.[11] In English, by contrast, the word *science* has been so thoroughly filled with the sense of empirical observation, accurate measurement, and verifiable statements that it seems strange, to say the least, and insane, to say the most, when theology is called "the science of God." It may not be worth the effort to justify a reclamation of the term *science* for theological purposes. What *is* worth establishing, however, is the fact that theological methods and the methods of what is generally termed science are not in fundamental opposition: as though the former were all subjective speculation and the latter all objective description. More and more it is recognized that the religious propensity for creating myths and models to express and convey what is "real" and "true" is matched by the scientific disposition to do the same.[12] Conversely, the disciplined obligation of scientists to concentrate maximum attention on empirical data—things given in reality—is incumbent also upon religious thinkers.

Both science and faith have the power to constitute particular communities of persons. There is a careless and growing habit of calling every kind of human grouping a community with spurious justification: scuba divers, funeral directors, oil drillers are called communities in a questionable sense. But scientists in general, and those in special fields, do have the shared interest, activity, and support which are the marks of authentic community. Thomas S. Kuhn observes:

> The members of a scientific community see themselves and are seen by others as the men uniquely responsible for the pursuit of a set of shared goals, including the training of their successors. Within such groups communication is relatively full and professional judgment relatively unanimous.[13]

The many scientific communities—state and national academies, national and international associations of particular disciplines—are much more than groupings of common interest. They reflect the constant cooperation and communication which are necessary for scientific and technological advance.

On the side of religious faith, of course, the communal character is generally taken for granted. The embodiment of Judaism in the Jewish people is fundamental; and Christianity in its beginning appropriated the Jewish concept of a special "people of God," albeit opened widely to Gentiles and Jews. To be a Jew in the religious sense and not belong to the people of the covenant is quite impossible. The same applies to individual Christians, who are by definition members of the church. Islam is an all-inclusive religious culture, often identified with a political state, as Christianity formerly was. Some Buddhists have recently adopted the form and even the name of "church" from Christianity. Distinctive religions such as Mormonism are tightly woven communities.

The purpose of showing the communal character of science and religion is to demonstrate their comparability. As often said in jest as well as sobriety, each has its hierarchical structure of authority, its priesthood and laity (though laymen for scientists are those outside the community). Both communities live off the patrimony of long traditions and the influence of their patriarchs and prophets, even while looking constantly for new truth to break forth into knowledge. The comparison can be extended as one thinks of their many common categories. Whereas the church calendar consists of holy days and the feasts of saints who have given shape to the Christian community over the centuries, the calendar published by *Science* magazine celebrates the birthdays of *its* saints: Kepler, Pasteur, von Neumann, and the like. Each calendar recognizes its accepted saints but not its rejected heretics. "In order to verify knowledge in science," says the Conference Report, "one has to commit oneself to the enterprise of science, become a member of the scientific community, and submit oneself to its discipline and its canons of inquiry." Likewise for religion: "Only committed and dedicated Christians in the community of a church can verify for themselves knowledge of the God and Father of our Lord Jesus Christ and the grace and power of his Holy Spirit."[14]

Language is not only an element of community but a decisive mark of the existence of each. Both science and theology keep reviewing, correcting, and augmenting their specialized vocabularies. Seemingly esoteric and obscure words by the hundreds are needed to give definitive expression to scientific and religious phenomena or concepts. Few persons come close to knowing the meaning of most chemical, medical, and physical words, or the many religious terms derived from Hebrew, Greek, Latin, Arabic, Sanskrit, Slavic, and Chinese roots. In addition, both kinds of community make regular use of nonverbal symbols, especially mathematical ones for the scientists.

Though language systems and symbols have communication as their purpose, their very complexity and quantity today tend to frustrate rather than ease the interchange of knowledge between religious and scientific communities. A rare person is the one who belongs to both and, in this sense, is bilingual.

Wang Hsien-Chih's fourth mark of comparison is that of belief or faith. These are just as implicit a part of science as they are explicit in religion. Some scientists would prefer to speak of presuppositions which give them confidence to proceed in experimentation and assessment. Even though the trust in fixed natural laws which govern all phenomena has been revised according to relativity theory and the principle of uncertainty, scientists still "walk by faith" as well as by seeing, hearing, smelling, and touching. The biblical description of faith as "the assurance of things hoped for, the conviction of things not seen," is not inappropriate to scientific attitude. As Paulos Gregorios of India, moderator of the Conference, compares science and religious faith, "both have an element of progress in understanding and practice, and have anticipations of a higher degree of perfection in both cognition of and relation to reality."[15]

FIVE WAYS OF RELATING SCIENCE AND FAITH

Half a century ago, Alfred North Whitehead spoke to his generation as other scientists might address ours in the new context: "When we consider what religion is for mankind, and what science is, it is no exaggeration to say that the future course of history depends upon the decision of this generation as to the relations between them."[16]

Are science and religious faith allies or adversaries? This is the overly simplistic—and therefore false—way of posing the question of relationship. Being comparable in structure does not limit their interface to a positive or negative stance. Indeed, at least five distinct kinds of relation are discernible as possibilities. There are many people, both the unlearned and the educated, who are adherents of each of the five positions. These may be delineated as: (1) mutual exclusion: dealing with separate dimensions of reality and experience; (2) mutual exclusion: seeing the same realities in differing ways; (3) interacting approaches to the same realities; (4) mutual dialectical interaction: keeping separate identity; (5) possible integration: complementarity by absorption or higher synthesis.

None of these, obviously, is of self-validating truth to every interested person. So it is worthwhile to consider what each implies for those who desire to clarify their own positions.[17]

Mutual Exclusion, Separate Realities

Single-minded dogmatists are found in both general communities: the ultraconservative Christian fundamentalists as well as mystics on one side, the positivists, or scientific materialists, on the other. Although they are at polar opposites in affirming what is real, true, and most important about life, they share the common attitude of dualism. They see two dimensions—one of reality and one of appearance; one of matter and one of spirit. These are always kept in separate mental compartments. The distinction is as old as philosophy itself ever since the thinkers and sages of Greece and India first pondered the significance of visible things and invisible ideas of divinity, morals, and aesthetics.

A religious person living in our present technological civilization may be persuaded that matter and things physical are real and useful, but that they have no bearing upon faith. What counts, and only counts, for human fulfillment and salvation is what can be adduced from the Bible and validated by passages of the text with chapter and verse. It is the Bible which describes the state of the world, whatever scientific observation and theory might try to say about it. Holding without question or reservation this fundamentalist position, an evangelistic preacher is quite aware of all the useful devices which science and technology provide. He lives in a house replete with products derived from the research of chemists, metallurgists, electrical engineers, pharmacologists, and nutritionists. He is awakened by a transistor clock-radio, shaves with stainless steel blades or electric shaver, dons clothes made of synthetic fibers, drives his fuel-injection car while the tape deck plays gospel music. At the church service, the electronic organ accompanies otherworldly hymns, service bulletins have been photocopied, and the King James translation (1603) of the Bible electrotyped. His sermon is a vigorous denunciation of everything "worldly" and commendation of what is "spiritual," using the text: "for the things which are seen are temporal, but the things which are not seen are eternal" (2 Cor. 4:18). As far as the East is from the West, so far are religion and science kept apart.

The scientific materialist is not just the mirror image of the Christian biblicist, however. If there is anything deserving the name reality, of course, it consists of matter, which is reducible to chemical elements and physical properties and energies. His materialistic outlook does not prevent him from being alert and sensitive to all kinds of immaterial phenomena known to human experience. He knows love for wife and children, ponders the mysteries of birth and death, enjoys the music of Vivaldi and Mahler, gives time to work against racial injustices in his city, and raises money to relieve malnutrition in Asia. As for religion, he professes none; but he is by no means a militant atheist. Some of his friends in the scientific community are believers, even (as often called) "active church members." But he dismisses their faith as a vestigial mental habit left over from the mores of a passing, prescientific culture. If they were honest and consistent in their scientific outlook, he thinks, they would agree with him that the religious claims for supersensory knowledge of supernatural reality are superseded by scientific observation and thus nullified.

Whereas the fundamentalist preacher does not, and cannot, deny the real presence of matter in his natural and artificial environment, the materialist cannot return the compliment by acknowledging any truth in religious confessions about the realm of spirit. "The impulse of the scientific attitude is the desire to learn," writes anthropologist George Gaylord Simpson, and continues, "to learn about ourselves, about others, about the earth, the universe. Its criterion is that what is learned should be real, should in fact exist in ourselves and outward into the universe." Then, noting the presence of religious ideas, he judges, "If a preacher says, 'We were created in the image of God,' the fact is that the preacher said it, and that is the only fact established."[18]

A meeting of minds is thus virtually ruled out for those who insist that scientific and religious facts or realities or phenomena have nothing in common. The philosopher Ludwig Wittgenstein has exercised great influence on contemporary thinkers by proposing his theory of "language games." Each sphere of interest has its own peculiar language, but they are not translatable from one to another. One can render Kant's German into French or Polish; but Einstein's mathematical symbols and Auden's poetry, or Stravinsky's musical scores and Kazantzakis's prose, are not reciprocally translatable. If the "language game" thesis suggests a way of speaking meaningfully about both science and religion without allowing any contact between them, this may appear to be a way of permitting reasonable discourse in each realm. But, as the Conference Report judges, this also "tends to trivialize both," for "it does not make clear how either can make true statements . . . and seems to degrade both science and faith into useful fictions."[19]

Mutual Exclusion, Same Realities

A switch of the first type of relationship might appear to bring science and faith into closer accord. This seems possible when people in both communities recognize that they are dealing with the same observed phenomena and data, rather than presupposing separate realms. In terms of nature, for example, the objects of attention are the origin of the universe and the earth, the beginnings of animate life, and the destiny of the cosmos. In human terms, the exemplary questions are the evolution and uniqueness of the human species, the function of the brain in relation to mind and self, to the experiences of pleasure, suffering and health, and to moral obligation. Since these are obviously questions of common occurrence to seriously thinking people and of profound significance, it might be assumed that all reflective persons of whatever religious and scientific views would be able to discuss them. But such exchange is foreclosed for people who declare resolutely that their community alone can engage in meaningful discourse about such matters. A most familiar debate is over cosmogony, or the origin of the earth. Conservative biblical theology requires an adamant defense of the account of creation given in the Book of Genesis. Never mind that the narrative bears resemblance to Babylonian creation mythology, which preceded the writing of Hebrew scriptures; the story must be defended and asserted as a factual description of what happened. And the defense is required for two related but not equally important reasons. The first is a defense of biblical truth. This is the uncompromising belief in the verbal inspiration and literal inerrancy of the Bible, which for many people is still the solid foundation of their faith. Once doubts of inerrancy are allowed, the whole structure of belief crumbles. The other, deeper, reason for intransigence is to protect belief in the absolute omnipotence and autonomy of God the Creator. If He is not the God who created the earth, the sun, moon, stars, flora, fauna, and Adam and Eve in the mode described, can He still be the God we worship and trust as the Preserver of the cosmos and Redeemer of humanity? If some scientific theories about creation, such as that of a steady state, or continuous creation of matter, can be seemingly reconciled to the biblical scenario, so much the better. But the traffic of such ideas must be one-way, not reciprocal; and the only permitted purpose is to appropriate support for the biblical doctrine. (It escapes the notice of some persons that no supports or assistance should be needed for a Bible which is self-authenticating or for a doctrine of God which is a priori true.)

Such fundamentalist belief determines a mode of thought which seems to be a throwback to the era of Copernicus, Bruno, and Galileo —those symbols of victimization by religious arrogance. Fortunately, the power of no Christian church or sect in our time is so strong or arbitrarily exercised that eminent scientists can be silenced, suppressed, or punished.

It takes at least two sides to make either an argument or a standoff. Is there a scientific counterpart to the kind of religious arrogance which has been described? Yes, it is widespread and generally respected in educated circles. Heard on a radio discussion was this statement: "You men of religion are motivated by religious faith, while we [scientists] are driven by the search for truth." The church representative on that panel responded with silence. Why? Concession? Cowardice? Or inability to say a credible word about a religious quest for truth?

One reason many scientists assume that dialogue with religious people would be at best fruitless and at worst impossible is because of their partial and prejudiced idea of what viewpoints and ideas are held by theologians and philosophers of religion. Exposed intermittently to the worst kinds of uninformed, uncritical religious declarations; steeped in the message of intolerance as conveyed symbolically by the Galileo tragedy; personally devoid of friends and colleagues who can speak with assurance and intelligence on theological ideas of nature, man, and God; committed by education and mature conviction to the epistemology of their scientific method; scientists of such experience and perspective may be expected to assume that dialogical meeting points with religious beliefs and insights are nonexistent.

At the close of his fascinating book *The First Three Minutes,* 1979 Nobel Laureate Steven Weinberg declares, "Men and women are not content to comfort themselves with tales of gods and giants . . . they also build telescopes and satellites and accelerators."[20] He does not say explicitly who the devotees of "gods and giants" are, but it is hardly possible in that context to avoid the implication that these are the benighted believers in a transcendent power of creation and purpose. Moreover, the pathos of this cavalier dismissal of nonscientific thought is emphasized on the same page by the sardonic observation that the human quest for knowledge is all that saves the whole cosmos from being a colossal "farce." "The more the universe seems comprehensible"—due to brilliant intellectual inquiry such as this—"the more it also seems pointless."

Between the kinds of religious and scientific attitudes which are mutually exclusive there is no intended, much less necessary, hostility or conflict. Their representatives simply look upon the same phenomena in totally different ways, with no expressed desire for interaction or reconciliation. Why is this? Perhaps, it is suggested, because the realms of faith (religious of whatever kind) and science (in all its variety) have their own nontranslatable languages. Even though they both purport to deal with the same problems of understanding the natural order and human existence, science and faith are, in this view, totally different systems of thought. Thus, it is not accurate to say, as above, that uncritical fundamentalism differs from scientific materialism, but that all religious schools are on one side of the chasm and all scientific views on the other.

Interacting Approaches to the Same Realities

The stereotypical religionist and scientist may be separated by the two distinct fields of interest which never touch, or else by two uncommunicable conceptions of what life and nature are about. Either cause of separation spells mutual exclusion; and both mean an enormously dangerous shattering of personal and societal integrity in this era of science-based technology.

Interaction is a better alternative, but this, too, comes in two styles. In one kind of interaction, conflict is the rule; in the other, interpenetration of questioning and resolution.

Religious and scientific interests meet and clash over the same kinds of issues: the origin of earth and species; the identity, behavior, and value of human life; the purpose of natural and human history in the great cosmic order. Instead of the coldly disdaining standoff, there is real engagement, disputation, and even provisional or lasting modification of arguments as minds really meet.

Military vocabulary has prevailed too long in the discussion of this relationship. For decades after Darwin's theories were introduced, studied, and debated, it was popularly assumed that a state of war existed between religion and science. "Crusades," "skirmishes," "setbacks," "victories" were the customary diction.[21] Such analogies are now obsolete: or if they have any residual sense, it might be said that a few straggling, retreating infantry of the religious forces are taking parting shots at the scientific enemy, which advances unopposed. More specifically, this means that the antievolutionists suffered defeat at the decisive battle of Dayton, Tennessee in 1925 (the Scopes trial) and have been generally discredited by the East African fossil discoveries of the palaeontologists Leakey and their co-workers.

The defeat of some religious forces was due not only to the overwhelming power of the sciences, however; equally effectual has been the relativizing of biblical authority caused by a century of critical scholarship affecting textual accuracy, translations, and theological interpretations. This means that the time has long passed since the main issues were the literal facticity of the creation of the earth in six twenty-four-hour working days, Adam's instantaneous creation as a mature man with Eve's body potential in his rib, Joshua's power to stop the movement of planets or Jonah's three-day resistance to the digestive juices of the whale. Conversely, the scientist who still chides theologians for speculating on the number of pin-head-dancing angels reveals both ignorance and bad manners. On the emptiness of these debates, the British scientist Mary Hesse, declares: "Science does *not* tell the way the world is in any sense fundamental enough to come into conflict with the necessary presuppositions of religion."[22]

How is it in the "postwar" era? Church leaders and theologians, by and large, have beaten their verbal swords into shares to plow new fields of knowledge. And once aggressive scientists have changed their iconoclastic spears into tools for pruning the dead branches of obsolescent ideas. For, according to the French writer André Dumas, the science-religion antagonism has begun to be a knowledge-wisdom dialogue.[23] To the sheer quantity of knowledge which scientists can still acquire there is no apparent limit. Do the same scientists, as participants in their larger community, possess the wisdom appropriate for deciding on the technical, social, and political uses of their research results? That is a matter of dispute among scientists themselves and with other members of society. Certainly, in the minds of some scientists, the sense of omnicompetence in their own fields is held in good conscience; neither in pride nor arrogance, they claim to have both knowledge and wisdom. This attitude of confidence concerning the wise uses of the genie of science is most important, and has been most challenged, in relation to military uses. The uninhibited militarist can now clap his hands and order the scientific genie to produce almost any material, device, or power. Poison gases of highest potency against all plant and animal life, biological weapons, laser beams, missiles and antimissiles under computerized command, and atomic weapons of literally inconceivable destructiveness—scientists who create them and condone their use either feel gratified and satisfied or else are plagued in conscience for having "known sin," as J. Robert Oppenheimer observed. In research, it might be said, they explored the mysteries of creation; in present military application they face the mysteries of destruction and damnation. Hardly less serious than martial considerations are those affecting natural ecological cycles, human environment, frivolous economic productivity, and the very character, genetic and physiological, of the human body.

André Dumas judges that the science community felt quite secure in wisdom and prudence until the end of the 1940s. It enjoyed unquestioning public approval and uncritical self-appraisal as it stood on the brink of its two most exciting and productive decades. In the same period, most Christian theological and ethical thinking was indifferent to scientific achievements and preoccupied with ecclesiastical and social issues.[24] When theologians in the 1960s were attracted to study questions of the philosophy of science and technology, most were too timid to make any significant contributions. In retrospect it would be quite wrong to say of recent decades that scientists have gained knowledge while religious philosophers and theologians have provided wisdom to aid in the implementation of knowledge. With demonstrable reason, Dumas believes that the time has now come when religious thinkers and scientists together and with equal respect, can carry on their dialogue and engage in common action for the good of humanity.

Mutual Interaction: Identities Retained

Good sense and fair play would seem to prescribe an amiable and constructive alliance between modern scientists and those responsible for religious teachings and activities. This could displace the previously described relationships of separateness and conflict, showing them to be intellectually inappropriate and culturally useless. Since science and religion as organized bodies of knowledge and wisdom are at the disposal of people of goodwill, intelligence, and civil responsibility, it should be evident that their utility will be magnified by their interaction. The distinctiveness and integrity of each discipline are neither blurred nor impugned by relating them so. As the theologian Hans Schwarz rightly observes:

> Though clashes between theology and the sciences have often occurred, they are unnecessary if each discipline remembers its own limits. By their very definition the sciences confine themselves to assertions about variations within the space-time and matter-energy continuum, while theology goes one step further by reflecting also on how this continuum was brought into existence and to whom it owes its structure.[25]

Schwarz's indication of the connection means that scientists and religious thinkers alike are interested in events and phenomena in the world, understanding them according to their learned competence and insight. The scientists clearly have the advantage here. But the questions of primordial cause and ultimate purpose, of aesthetic value and moral significance must also be addressed.

To answer these questions, scientists may attend to the words of theologians, philosophers, social scientists, and artists (though certain scientists are able simultaneously to assume other roles as well).

The endeavor of space travel serves to illustrate the occasion for

51

interaction. The culminating event was seen on television in 1969: men walking on the moon. How did they get there? And what was the significance of the lunar landing? From the minds, blackboards, drafting boards, laboratories, observatories, testing grounds, and shops of thousands of scientists came the required ingredients of the event. Astrophysics, chemistry, electronics, aerodynamics, metallurgy, computer science, optics, and meteorology were just some of the major divisions of science engaged in the effort. To the technologies derived from them were related, indispensably, the decisive factors of social sciences: the political reasons for undertaking the huge project and the economic resources derived from taxation and disbursed as rewards to contracted industries and their employees and stockholders. With imagination one can think of numerous other pieces in this vast mosaic of scientific enterprise. As Donald Glen Ivey, Professor of Physics, University of Toronto, said of the American moon shot:

> All of the scientific effects are peripheral. This is primarily political; it is also now, because of such big business, economic. And the scientific effects are small. The amount of the budget involved that can be considered in any way scientific is certainly less than ten percent.[26]

Where was the interaction with religion? It was reported that one astronaut carried a gold Star of David, a St. Christopher medal, and a Crucifix—all three for good luck.

Another, sensing communion with the Creator of the cosmos, read back to earthlings the familiar words of Genesis, to the chagrin of aggressive atheists and the comfort of believers. "In the beginning God" eventually appeared as the motto on the commemorative postage stamp.

And not to be forgotten, people everywhere prayed for the safety of the moonwalkers.

These religious affections did not amount to interaction, however. To whatever degree they were expressions of sincere faith in the creative and providential God, they were still only pious glosses on the event. Interaction and interpenetration of thought are both more important and more complex. They were, and still are, considered in pondering such questions as the following:

1. What is the enlarged insight into the nature and value of the species *homo sapiens* that is capable of so prodigious an achievement?

2. Are such intelligence and skill the result of random chemical occurrence, or the consequence and reflection of divine mind? What is the difference for understanding human behavior?

3. Does the event provide strong evidence of the progressive evolution of the human race in both intellect and mastery of nature, indicating ever-improving development?

4. Does the plain fact that humans are no longer confined to the earth (Soviet cosmonauts have stayed up for months already!) point to the likelihood of cognate forms of life elsewhere in this galaxy?

5. Was the lunar shot better interpreted as America's extravagant ostentation in competition with the Soviet Union? The Stars and Stripes were planted on the moon's surface, of course.

6. Acknowledging the moral concern, profoundly exemplified by Jesus Christ as a divine mandate, for the well-being of each human being, must we regret, or condemn, the space program as immoral waste of resources?

7. Is human will generally so corrupt that the consequences of this achievement will take the form mainly of military technology?

Often it is said that the interaction of science and religion is possible because of their complementarity. This means that what is lacking in one is found in the other, so each supplies something needed for the completion of the other. Is it a valid concept? Probably not. It has the virtue of avoiding both separateness and conflict and of suggesting cooperation. The idea might also enable religious believers who are scientifically disposed to avoid a kind of mental schism. Nevertheless, complementarity is a misleading idea,[27] because it leads into the unsatisfactory notion of "the God of the gaps." This is the deceptively attractive belief that a reference to God can serve to answer perplexing questions which science cannot answer. To be sure, there are questions, especially of origin and destiny, which scientists cannot explain and about which there are biblical and theological doctrines. The doctrines of creation and eschatology are, according to faith, true. But their truth is not of the same order as scientific theories of cosmology, entropy, or their variations. This leads us to ask, not entirely facetiously, whether there may be a "science of the gaps" to fill in the lacunae of theological understanding.

Dialectical interaction, then, remains a preferred mode of describing a relationship which is congenial and cooperative, but cautiously critical of easy resolutions of intractable problems of thought, investigation, and faith.

Possible Integration: Unification or Absorption?

Wherever there is a thesis opposed by an antithesis, a follower of Hegelian thought will design a synthesis. Synthesizing is most consonant with the ideal of rational order as cherished and sought by many intellectuals. Antitheses and conflicts suggest an absurdity or a contradiction in the nature of things. But if nature, or the earth and universe, are held to be complex manifestations of an eternal unity, then ways are sought in human experience to overcome discordant oppositions by higher, unifying syntheses.

Because of their devotion to the unity of truth, therefore, some people look for, and hope for, the integration of the sciences and religions of humankind into a comprehensive whole. This is clearly different from the dialectical interaction, which yet leaves the two realms to their proper functions.

In chemical synthesis two or more elements become one substance. When science and religion are heated in the glass retort, so to speak, it is most likely that one will just absorb the other and integrate it into itself. Some religions presume to absorb science: for example, Scientology, several "religious science" cults, and Western theosophies with roots in Yoga and Hindu philosophy. Dumas criticizes such types of religion, ancient or modern, which "confuse the uniqueness of God with the unity of the universe . . . [since] the Bible speaks of the unique God and not of the divine One, which risks always devaluing the multiple, while on the contrary the unique God values the disconcerting variety and complexity of creation."[28]

In a way—it is frequently charged—Pierre Teilhard de Chardin attempted to do the same thing by appealing, not to the cosmic monism of Oriental religious thought, but to the cosmic Christology of Christian faith. In his very appealing mystical view, the history of creation is like a cone-shaped movement: all matter and life, including evolving intelligent human life, move toward the ultimate "omega-point" of destiny. Reaching that point, the race becomes the Christ and creation returns to the Creator, who is "all in all."

Has Teilhard's thought thus integrated science and faith? The debate goes on. But among his severe critics is George Gaylord Simpson, who rejects this accommodation of science to religion. Such "efforts to combine science and religion may be noble in intention but usually end up distorting or stultifying both," he writes. In Teilhard's writing, "the evolutionary principles are distorted and downright falsified for seeming coherence with the non-scientific, non-naturalistic premises. In turn, the mystical views advanced as having that false basis are thereby vitiated."[29] The British Nobel Laureate in physiology and medicine, Sir Peter Medawar, dismisses Teilhard's writing as just an "enthusiastic but largely incoherent rhapsody."[30]

It is questionable whether science in general, or particular scientific disciplines, can be baptized into a religion. Instead, some seek to immerse Christian faith in science and thereby achieve an integration.

It is widely acknowledged that the biblical view of creation (or nature) and the emphasis upon intellectual freedom, both taught by Christianity, encouraged the rise of modern science in Europe. This encouragement was combined, incidentally, with strong influences from Arabic sciences; the philosophies of ancient Greece, which Italians of the fifteenth century devoured along with rediscovered paganism, also gave impetus to the new scientific mentality.[31] Today it seems to be assumed by some that Christian faith, having assisted science to develop in past centuries, should be conformed to the knowledge which the scientific community claims to have. It often happens that individual scientists exchange their inherited Christian religion for views which are labeled scientific humanism, scientism, or scientific materialism. If there is to be an integration, or synthesis, of faith with these positions, let it be by assimilation of faith into the thought world of science, they say.

As men and women become educated, develop into maturity, and assume social responsibilities, they cannot avoid the challenges of both faith and science. Of course, they can respond, if they will, with a know-nothing shrug of shoulders and extension of open hands. (As Edwin Newman relates the ultimate jargon of ignorance, "Ya know, ya never know.") So much for immaturity at whatever age. But for those of normally developed mind, the mysteries and revelations explored by religion and science require a response, an attitude. And in this chapter some brief indicators of the possible options have been discussed.

Which of them is most satisfactory as a way toward further learning and enlightened faith? The Conference Report clearly favors the fourth: mutual interaction. "In the midst of this intellectual ferment in both science and technology . . . in science and Christianity in different ways, it is a vision of a wider truth and coherence which lies within our reach, if each could find a way to free itself from the sterile conflicts and protective armor of its past relationships with the other."[32]

NOTES

1. The historian of science, Stanley L. Jaki, has demonstrated how Christian faith and scientific inquiry have been compatible and mutually supportive in the thinking of many leading scientists from the sixteenth century through the present; "Theological Aspects of Creative Science," *Creation, Christ and Culture*, ed. Richard W. A. McKinney (Edinburgh: T. & T. Clark, 1976), pp. 149–66; also, Jaki, *Science and Creation* (New York: Science History Publications, 1974), chap. 12.

2. Enrico Cantore, *Scientific Man* (New York: Institute for Scientific Humanism, 1977), p. 131.

3. "Address of Pope John Paul II," *Science*, 207 (March 14, 1980): 1166. The address to the Pontifical Academy of Sciences, Vatican City, November 10, 1979.

4. Norbert Wiener, *God and Golem, Inc.* (Cambridge: M.I.T. Press, 1964), p. 47.

5. William Barrett, *The Illusion of Technique* (Garden City: Anchor Press, 1978), pp. 105–6.

6. Bertrand Russell, *Mysticism and Logic* (London: Arnold, 1929), pp. 47–48.

7. Francis Crick, *Of Molecules and Men* (Seattle: University of Washington Press, 1966), p. 93.

8. Edward O. Wilson discerns self-sacrificing behavior in favor of others of the species, especially kin, in many animal species as a consequence of genetic conditioning. He applies this same explanation to altruistic behavior of human beings, although not in a fully deterministic way. *Sociobiology, The New Synthesis* (Cambridge: Harvard University

Press, 1975), pp. 3–4, 117–29; also *On Human Nature* (Cambridge: Harvard University Press, 1978), pp. 152–65. See J. Robert Nelson, "A Theologian's Response to Wilson's *On Human Nature*," *Zygon* 15 (1980).

9. Wang Hsien-Chih, address to Science Students' Conference, Wellesley College, Wellesley, Mass., July 1979.

10. Robert K. Merton, *The Sociology of Science* (Chicago: University of Chicago Press, 1973), pp. 275–78.

11. Wolfhart Pannenberg, *Theology and the Philosophy of Science*, trans. Francis McDonagh (Philadelphia: Westminster Press, 1976), pp. 297–300.

12. See, for example, Ian G. Barbour, *Myths, Models and Paradigms* (New York: Harper & Row, 1974).

13. Thomas S. Kuhn, *The Structure of Scientific Revolutions*, 2d ed. (Chicago: University of Chicago Press, 1970), p. 177.

14. *Faith and Science in an Unjust World*, vol. 2 (Philadelphia: Fortress Press, 1980), p. 18.

15. Paulos Gregorios, "Science and Faith: Complementary or Contradictory?" *Faith and Science*, vol. 1, p. 53. On the scientists' elements of faith see Robert D. Clark, *Science and Christianity, a Partnership* (Mountain View: Pacific Press, 1972), pp. 78–82; Harold K. Schilling, "Toward the Confluence of the Scientific and Christian Faiths," *Zygon*, 4 (1969).

16. Alfred North Whitehead, *Science and the Modern World* (New York: Free Press, 1953), p. 181.

17. The five kinds of relationship described here differ somewhat from those in the Report of Section I, The Nature of Science and the Nature of Faith (*Faith and Science*, vol. 2, pp. 7–27). Similar discussions are found in the journal *Zygon*: Harold H. Oliver, "The Complementarity of Theology and Cosmology," 13 (1978), in which he delineates the three relationships of conflict, compartment, and complementarity; Hugo Adam Bedau, "Complementarity and the Relation between Science and Religion," 9 (1974), pp. 202–4; D. M. McKay, "Complementarity in Scientific and Religious Thinking," 9 (1974), p. 225.

18. George Gaylord Simpson, *Concession to the Improbable* (New Haven: Yale University Press, 1978), p. 28.

19. *Faith and Science*. vol. 2, p. 16.

20. Steven Weinberg, *The First Three Minutes* (New York: Basic Books, 1977), p. 155.

21. A full treatment of the "warfare" between Darwinians and the religiously motivated anti-Darwinians is found in James R. Moore, *The Post-Darwinian Controversies* (New York: Cambridge University Press, 1979).

22. Mary Hesse, *Anticipation*, 25 (January 1979): 9.

23. André Dumas, "Evolution in the Social Ethic of the World Coun-

cil Since Geneva 1966," *The Manipulated Man.* ed. Franz Böckle (New York: Herder & Herder, 1971), p. 127.

24. André Dumas, "Evaluation of the Ecumenical Encounter between Theologians and Scientists," *Anticipation,* 22 (May 1976): 33.

25. Hans Schwarz, *Our Cosmic Journey* (Minneapolis: Augsburg Publishing House, 1977), p. 151.

26. Donald Glen Ivey, *Science and Conscience* (Toronto: Canadian Broadcasting Corporation, 1968), p. 58.

27. Ian G. Barbour uses complementarity in a strict sense within the field of physics, as wave and particle models are described by Niels Bohr, *Myths,* p. 78. See also Harold H. Oliver, "Complementarity," and John Dillenberger, *Protestant Thought and Natural Science* (New York: Doubleday, 1960), p. 287.

28. André Dumas, "Evaluation of the Ecumenical Encounter," p. 35.

29. George Gaylord Simpson's words from *Meaning of Evolution* (rev. ed., 1967) are quoted with approval in the article "Philosophy of Nature," *Encyclopaedia Brittanica,* 15th ed.

30. P. B. Medawar and J. S. Medawar, *The Life Science: Current Ideas in Biology* (New York: Harper and Row, 1977), p. 168.

31. Stanley L. Jaki, *Science and Creation,* gives a detailed evaluation of these and other influences on science.

32. *Faith and Science,* vol. 2, pp. 19–20.

3 | Nature, Nature's God, and God's Image in Humanity

ASSAULTS ON NATURE
ARE HUMAN SELF-DESTRUCTION

If it is the proper business of science to explain the processes of nature, it is that of religious faith to express values and purposes as humanly perceived. Recognizing this division of function, persons representing each can meet, disagree, agree, cooperate, and enrich their own knowledge and wisdom. This is what interaction implies. But easily attained cooperation and harmony cannot always be expected. In one such meeting in Bucharest, 1974,[1] people of diverse sciences and theologies agonized over a major cause of contradiction and uncertainty. The cause was, and remains, the global ecological danger. The question: by what right or justification do human beings make unrestrained and arbitrary use of the rest of nature? By nature is generally meant the earth's whole store of animal species, plants, and minerals. In Christian terms nature is equivalent to all the terrestrial creation—and in this day—the moon as well.

For many people this is a nonquestion, or one which has a self-evident answer. Put ironically, does a bird need a right to eat a worm or insect? Must it ask a Divine Bird for permission to build a nest in a certain place? Does it express thanks to the divinity for these allowances? To be "free as a bird" means, by analogy, that we are free in nature to do as we will and can. So many people have thought for centuries. Human beings need daily food, as well as materials to fashion or consume in their irrepressible drive to develop culture. Who can reasonably question this?

The reasonable and insistent question arises whenever human error,

59

stupidity, avarice, and fecundity despoil the earth and threaten its non-renewable resources. That time is now, and the spoliation is everywhere. To describe the global situation adequately would strain the limits of good taste in the use of superlative adjectives: the most, the greatest, the worst!

People of sense and responsibility, who do not choose to act as though theirs is the last surviving generation in history, cannot avoid the feeling of shame and anxiety for our race's assaults upon this earth, which is our only home. But the possession of faith in the creative and moral God, or the lack of it, determines how people think about the manifest crisis. The degree of intensity of shame and anxiety, and of determination to reverse the destructive trend, is not necessarily dependent upon theistic faith or its alternative beliefs, and ideologies. But the faith can provide a motivation of particular cogency because faith is inseparable from love and hope.

Those of a rigorously and exclusively scientific world view are seeking explanations and resolutions of ecological problems in a variety of areas of thought: psychology, ethics, technology, economics, and politics. By what psychological categories can behavior which destroys a good environment be explained? Or, conversely, the behavior which sustains and improves it? How are matters of right and wrong, altruism and selfishness, greed and restraint to be resolved in favor of constructive actions? From these problems comes the question of whether the powerful currents of economic interest and political power can serve positive ends. That is, can they cause technological methods and devices to be deployed in ways which will minimize pollution and conserve natural resources while still serving human needs? As long as the dominant economic motive is to gain the most profit in the shortest time, industries which deplete resources and corrupt environment will continue to cause damage to the earth and human society. As long as the mainspring of political action is for politicians to win the next election—or succeed in the next coup d'etat—the problems of ecological attrition will be unattended. The alternatives to these motivations and objectives can obviously be pressed upon people of power only by a combination of strong moral concern for human welfare and full recognition of the world's imminent perils.

Most evidently, we want to survive individually, as families, and as a race. Those few who wish for their own demise, or who speculate with equanimity upon the annihilation of the race, either have a disposition toward melancholia, or know they have reached the limits of endurance, or are the victims of a mental pathology. Most would agree that survival for an individual's full life span or for the race's continuity is not a goal which represents the loftiest aspiration of the human spirit. At the least, we human beings have this purpose in common with all living species, most of which seem content to find food and reproduce. A great many individuals neither reproduce nor survive, however, because they are food for other species. One can miss the intent of the Hebrew psalmist—which is to praise God—if one expresses a cynical remark about the psalmist's prayer:

> The eyes of all look to thee,
> and thou givest them their food in due season.
> Thou openest thy hand,
> thou satisfiest the desire of every living thing.
> (Ps. 145:15–16)

The singer of praises to the God of a small pastoral nation could honestly declare such gratitude. But when more than three billion people are looking not only for "food in due season" but all the amenities of living in a technological civilization, the opening hand of the Lord is a poetic figure for the resources, both fixed and renewing, of the earth itself. Were we three billion, or four, hunters and gatherers—such as the bushmen of the Kalahari desert land—we would already have depleted the planet of natural food. Instead, we are tillers, planters, harvesters, breeders, and fishers; and we know well enough how we can enable the good earth (as the hand of the Lord) to feed us. But what we know of food production is different from what we do, or fail to do, in order to use the earth effectively. Not only do we fail as a race to feed everyone, but we recklessly assault soil, water, air, and ecological systems in such ways as to jeopardize our future productivity even more.

Barry Commoner, who has long been at the front of the movement for conservation, is not one of the sensational doomsdayers who predict the end of humanity before the year 2000. Weighing the melancholy announcements of the end, he observes, more moderately but very seriously, "the present course of environmental degradation, at least in industrialized countries . . . is so serious that, if continued, it will destroy the capability of the environment to support a reasonably civilized human society."²

Animals are content only to survive. But human beings hope, and that is a major critical distinction. The hope for realizing the fullness of selfhood and personality within communities and nations leads us more and more to consume the natural resources which we consider requisite to that realization. Clearly, survival is the first prerequisite of hope.

The greater the need to consume, the greater the temptation to acquisitiveness and greed. These selfish passions have a way of feeding themselves. Satisfactions of desires for food, comfort, amusement, and power are only temporary. As experience has shown in millions of instances, satisfactions seem to create new desires. "I will build bigger barns," said the rich farmer to himself in Jesus' parable of human greed. In present terms this means bigger refrigerators, more and more electrical gadgets, more and richer food, finer cars, more highways and parking lots, more comforts of cooling and heating, more financial investments, more entertainment and sensate distraction. Always more! The high living style, to which most people in all countries aspire, and many enjoy, keeps breeding its own insatiable wants. The poor are not lacking in such desires because of their modest and ascetic attitudes, but unlike the relatively rich and richer, the poor have lacked the opportunity, the drive, the talent, or the good luck to attain a self-multiplying prosperity.

Acquiescence to greedy appetite may seem to be justified and encouraged by two kinds of perversion of philosophical and religious outlook. One is the hedonistic notion that we human beings live only for transitory enjoyment. So get it while you can! In a distorted manner we obey Jesus' counsel, "take no thought for the morrow," because we are using up everything we like from day to day. Today's gratification becomes tomorrow's stimulation to have more. On the ecological implications of hedonistic greed, the Edinburgh biologist C. H. Waddington assumed the prophet's mantle and charged in vehement tone that the "malpractices which have been brought back from America" have caused the increase of pollution in Europe.

It is, I would argue, the worship of Mammon the Almighty Dollar, not Science which has to bear the blame. It is Greed, Get Rich Quick, Turn a Quick Buck, Mine that Soil, Get Your Hands on That Gold, Squeeze Those Bastards Out, Control the Market, that provides the demonic drive to turn God's Own Country into God's Own Junk Yard. And the pseudopsycho-analytical double-talk about all this . . . is more than I can swallow.[3]

The other cause for hedonistic recklessness in the destructive uses of environment is often disguised as religious piety. It is the belief that "the earth with its store of wonders untold" is not simply there for our taking, but that the Creator has given it to us to do with as we will. If we think that we are the Elect among "all people that on earth do dwell," we can also believe that the dominion which Yahweh gave us through Adam really means license to dominate and exploit everything on land or in the sea. It is amazing how the burgeoning literature on anxiety about ecology shows that the saga of creation in Genesis keeps asserting its influence on thought and attitude, but in both benign and deleterious ways. It is fruitless for conservation-minded Christians to pretend that the words of domination are not in the biblical text. They are there. The question is just how in our present situation we choose to apply them.

Our primal ancestor was commanded by his Creator to "subdue" the earth (Gen. 1:28). Well, does that not make divinely legitimate the leveling of forests for needed timber and arable land, the extracting of soil fertility, and the least costly ways of getting metals and fossil fuels from the earth? Adam was also ordered to "have dominion over the fish of the sea . . . birds of the air . . . and every living thing that moves upon the earth" (1:28). So, it is believed, the benign providence of "nature and nature's God" allows humans to slaughter animals for their furs and horns, harpoon whales and seals for oil, and hunt birds and wild animals, not for food, but for the sport and fun of it. That "God-fearing people" have felt, and still feel, privileged to do these things cannot be denied. The much disputed question, discussed below, is whether the biblical idea of "dominion" is the chief cause of the world's ecological and environmental crisis. A lately deceased maharajah in India might have been asked how he justified his boast of having shot two thousand tigers, presumably without encouragement from the words of Genesis. In short, if the ruthless pillaging of natural nonhuman life and inert resources is largely due to an imprudent desire to satisfy all our wants, can the destructive urge be sanctioned and even ratified by an appeal to the biblical teaching on creation?

The drive for survival and the exercise of greedy impulses may seem overly simplistic as explanations of humanity's inhuman treatment of nature. If so, a third cause presents itself. This is the unintended spoliation which results from errors of judgment, miscalculation, and unavoidable misfortunes. Many examples of inadvertent damage come to mind in which people who effected it need not be blamed or held responsible. They were doing what they thought right and lawful in both civil courts and the court of creation.

Early hunters, explorers, and pioneer settlers in the western expanses of Canada and America saw vast herds of bison and elk, forests filled with animals, rivers and lakes alive with great bass and trout, beaver and otter, geese, ducks, and beautiful birds of all varieties. They saw forests in virgin estate, extending far beyond their range of vision, plains of black soil as yet uncut by plows. Immigrants who came from Britain and Europe to Africa, Australia, and South America saw comparable sights. Theirs was an experience which can never again be enjoyed. But they must have assumed that these rich resources were of virtually infinite quantity. Frontiersman and historian Francis Parkman described in *The Oregon Trail* how he shot the buffalo, or bison, by the hundreds in 1847. Some he shot just because they looked "too ugly to live." "Thousands of the bulls might be slaughtered without causing any detriment to the species," he wrote, "for their numbers greatly exceed those of the cows."[4] How could these pioneers have thought otherwise? Or how could they have imagined that two future factors would hasten the depletion of the seemingly inexhaustible riches? First, the vastly multiplied numbers of people who would occupy the planet. Second, the technological efficiency of machines and chemicals for harvesting, destroying, and killing. Only in retrospect can the extent of the damage be measured. And the new movements of citizens and governments for conservation and replenishment are too tardy to dress the earth's wounds.

Can the people responsible for manufacturing and keeping public order during the recent half century also be excused for ignorance of the possible consequences of expanding technology? Only recently, for example, has the poisoning power of chemicals become recognized, understood, and dreaded. Their identity and number can scarcely be cataloged, but the public has at least come to know about them. DDT, carbon monoxide, carbon dioxide, mercury and lead compounds, strontium 90, phosphates, nitrites, dioxin, ENU, PCB—ordinary people need not be chemists to know these names of toxic compounds, because they are mentioned in the newspapers almost daily now. Already the time has come, the time predicted by some prophets only twenty years ago, when radios must warn city dwellers with respiratory ailments that the air pollution has reached the level of real danger. In Europe, not only are the waters of great rivers unfit to drink, but such beautiful shores and beaches as those of Lake Geneva and the Mediterranean Sea are posted against swimming. Bangkok, once a most lovely and exotic Asian city of canals, has within twenty years virtually succumbed to water and air pollution.

In estimated gross numbers, out of more than five million species of insects, some hundreds of thousands are in real danger of extinction. And of the earth's quarter of a million species of plants, hundreds share the same peril. These threats, now virtually irreversible and certain, are due not only to the reckless use of insufficiently tested chemicals but also to the destruction of temperate woodlands, tropical rain forests, wetlands, and grasslands. The symbiosis of many combinations of plants, insects, and aquatic life is so well-known that we may imagine many others, as yet undiscovered, which are indispensable to nature's balanced life cycles.

Now, the human race generally, and particular people, are not blameless for these and similar horrendous happenings. But the blame is due to ignorance or avarice rather than to premeditated assault upon nature. Neither can the blame easily or justly be charged to the Christian faith for its alleged teaching of irresponsible domination. It is certainly not the first chapter of Genesis which skippers of colossal oil tankers have in mind when their ships collide and spill crude oil by the thousands of tons. Nor is it reasonable to call Christianity culpable when men in Asia and Africa kill a rhinoceros for the awesome horn with its legendary power of aphrodisiac stimulation—for this also is ignorance.

In a class by itself is modern militarism as a cause for environmental pollution and destruction. Militarism today does not mean just infantry armed with rifles and combat pilots chasing enemies in the air. It means the massive mobilization of great technological systems as developed by the largest nations which belong to the exclusive Nuclear Club.

Even before the awesome decision is made about employing bombs and missiles with their atomic payloads, measured in units of a million-tons-of-TNT-explosive-power (a megaton), the annihilating force of conventional weapons is ruining the environment as well as maiming and killing people. Napalm fires become infernos in a split second, consuming everything and everyone. In the war in Vietnam, American forces used these hellish fires as conventional weapons. Likewise, the herbicide dioxin, called Agent Orange, not only defoliated and poisoned great areas of land in Vietnam, but may have been a weapon against American personnel themselves. In addition to the "scorched earth" which resulted, soldiers who were exposed to the chemical eventually suffered neurological trauma, begat children impaired by genetic mutations, developed malignant cancers, and died untimely deaths. A decade later these war veterans claim they can legally sue the chemical manufacturers for personal damages and receive compensatory payments from the government which sent them to Vietnam. Experimentation with still more toxic compounds continues to point toward increasing perils.

Yet the dangers of chemicals of whatever toxicity are surpassed by those of atomic weapons. Even short of exploding nuclear devices in warfare, the examples of radioactive fallout from testing and putative radiation from nuclear energy plants have shown the world what it has to fear.

The current debate over how to salvage and protect terrestrial ecology is pressed vigorously for various reasons. It is not simply a two-sided debate, but many-sided. If it were a game and a gamble, we could justly say that no stakes have ever been higher for the people of the whole world. There are economic considerations of incalculable amounts and political interests which can affect the future of nations, as well as agricultural, hydrological, and energy factors which can spell life or death for many millions. Underlying the whole concern is the problem of understanding philosophically the relationships which the United Nations Educational, Scientific, and Cultural Organization calls "Man and the Biosphere" and which theologians designate "God, humanity and all creation."

RELIGION IN ECOLOGICAL CONCERN

Does religion really have anything to do with this precarious condition of the planet? Probably less than its advocates claim, and more than its detractors allow.

When the whole earth has become a foul Augean Stable, the Herculean task of cleaning it falls to the whole race. Insofar as the United Nations symbolizes humanity at large, this task *is* being assumed.

Following the United Nations Conference on the Human Environment—Stockholm 1972, "Only One Earth"[5]—the international anxiety level was raised. With headquarters in Nairobi, the United Nations Environmental Program (UNEP) is commissioned to keep an "earth watch" on the most serious areas of depletion, pollution, and desertification. Other UN agencies, such as UNESCO and the World Health Organization, also share the concern. They remind people that much more than a cleanup is needed. What is necessary as well is a change of understanding and attitude with respect to humanity and nature: a change from an attitude of defensiveness, aggressiveness, and exploitation to one of respect and cooperation. Thus the economic motives of rich industrial nations must be modified to account for assistance to the poor ones in preserving their own environments and using their resources for developing agriculture, industry, and commerce. Health maintenance, meaning the enhancement of physical well-being for the sake of human fulfillment and productivity, is also a major dimension of the ecological problem.

It is unlikely that an unambiguous, practical, and universally applicable theory of ecological management can be deduced from the varieties of religious traditions. In general, Hindu and Buddhist attitudes are expressed in the teaching of nonviolence.[6] This may be attributed partly to the prevailing Asiatic sense of unity between humanity and nature. It is experienced by millions of people in their daily intimacy with the soil and with animal life, and expressed convincingly in traditional artistic motifs. However, nature pictured in Oriental art is seldom in the raw, but is rather like a tended garden inconspicuously occupied by men and women. In addition, the pervasive belief in transmigration of souls, metempsychosis or reincarnation, serves still as a powerful protection to many species of animals. In Hindu and Buddhist cultures there has been no lack of technical and architectural skill, of which many examples abound. Likewise, under the ancient influence of the Confucian philosophy of accommodation to nature, scientific and technical development in China was flourishing while Europe was still populated only by barbarous tribes. Asian science did not produce a technological eruption to compare to the Western industrial revolution with all its benefits and blights. The eminent historian of Chinese science, Joseph Needham, concedes that it was the lack of a theological conception of the creative, purposeful God of history which kept Oriental science and technology at a limited level of achievement.[7] Suddenly in the twentieth century Western technology has been imposed upon Oriental culture, the religions of which are quite unprepared for the cataclysmic changes.

The Muslim world experiences a similar problem. The notable scientific achievements of the Arabic cultures peaked a millennium ago, then suffered abrupt decline, while the Christian culture of Europe was in scientific ascendancy. Science and modern technology have only recently returned to the Muslim peoples of Western Asia, Indonesia, and North Africa. "In Islamic society," observes Fouad Zakaria, philosopher of Kuwait University, "where scientific values are still far from prevailing, the problem is: how can science justify itself in a society dominated by religious values?"[8] The traditional Islamic world view of a unified and harmonious cosmos, directly governed by Allah, has not, or not yet, been challenged by the pretensions of Western science and technology. The fierce resistance of Muslim leaders to Westernization is well-known in current events, even while the custodians of fabulous profits from oil sales are spending them on technological innovations for their countries. And as for a "theology of ecology," Zakaria explains that "problems of the environment are hardly felt in most Islamic societies, and hence rarely attract the attention of Moslem thinkers."[9]

It is to the biblical theological tradition of Judaism and Christianity that we must again refer in the quest for a religious interpretation of the widely believed conviction that human beings enjoy a distinct and definable relation to the Creator God, on the one hand, and the created world, or nature, on the other. The biblical ideas of creation are free from tribal, ethnic, or national exclusivism. They are archaic and largely mythological, but even today have an extraordinary effect upon discussions of humanity and nature. People who consider religion and theology as a whole to be mythical nevertheless find the biblical saga useful for rhetorical purposes. This may well be so because ideas such as our being, "made in the image of God," having "dominion" over animals, "subduing, tilling, and keeping the earth" are archetypal and fundamental. These narratives of Genesis are addressed to problems which are necessarily pondered by people of all cultures, religions, and nationalities. The early Mayans and Aztecs, Chinese of the Middle Kingdom, Bulgarians, Zulus, Dravidians, and Eskimos have had to decide how they are related to the land, plants, and animals around them, and to invisible forces both planetary and transcendent. Herein lie the bases of mythologies, sagas, astrology, religions, and—indeed—sciences. Confronted first by the world's mystery, humans sought its mastery. Ancient Greek and Roman philosophers, both Aristotelian and Stoic, believed in the subservience of animals and nonsentient nature to human mastery. They did not have an authoritative Bible or a monotheistic doctrine of creation to guide their thought. But the classical thinkers recognized the preeminence of humans, as both reasoners and fabricators, over the other living things of the earth.[10]

History shows clearly that the theology of creation, as originated in ancient Jewish faith and appropriated by Christianity, has been the matrix of thought wherein the highest degree of mastery over nature has been achieved. Is it only the matrix, or the compelling cause, for an exercise of mastery which is alarmingly destructive?

Few journal articles have provoked so much controversy as that of historian Lynn White, "The Historical Roots of Our Ecological Crisis." It must be discussed here, even though so familiar to many persons. As a defender of environment and a plaintiff against the biblical teaching, White places Genesis in the dock and accuses it of causing present troubles:

What did Christianity tell people about their relations within the environment? . . . Man named all the animals, thus establishing his dominance over them. God planned all this explicitly for man's benefit and rule: no item in the physical creation had any purpose save to serve man's purposes. And, although man's body is made of clay, he is not simply part of nature: he is made in God's image. Especially in its Western form, Christianity is the most anthropocentric religion the world has seen. . . . Hence we shall continue to have a worsening ecologic crisis until we reject the Christian axiom that nature has no reason for existence save to serve man.[11]

However much White may lack critical care in his exegesis, his charge is unequivocally direct. Is it also justified?

Admittedly true is the fact that the words used in Genesis are strong and harsh. In Gen. 1:26 and 28 the word *dominion* translates the Hebrew *rādāh – trample* and *kabas – tread down*. Other English translations and paraphrases are *master, take command, be dominator and king*. The same words, or their equal, are used in the famous "What is man?" Psalm:

> Thou has given him dominion over the works of thy hands;
> thou hast put all things under his feet.
>
> (Ps. 8:5)

At this citation in the courtroom, White might shout, "What more evidence do you need? The Bible is guilty!" But his argument in the article is neither so direct nor grossly simplistic. What he says is not that Christians are dominant destroyers of nature in contrast to scientists who deal responsibly with nature. Instead, he claims, as many do, that modern Western science "was cast in the matrix of Christian theology," receiving impetus from the "dynamism of religious devotion, shaped by Judaeo-Christian dogma of creation." Then science conceived and brought forth technology, and the two became the most effective means of assaulting nature, insofar as humans using them considered their "dominion" to be license for action.

But White's essay is flawed in two important respects. First, he oversimplifies and overstates his thesis, ignoring the many other influences besides religion which cause people to plunder natural resources. Second, he fails to demonstrate concretely how those phrases in Gen. 1:26 and 28 have directly influenced persons, groups, or whole societies to commit ecological outrages. In a subsequent article, White illustrates some ways in which Latin Christianity of the medieval era prized technology, but he adduces hardly enough evidence to support his thesis. While his argument is intelligible and plausible if true, it is not true just because he asserts it with much confidence.

A German theologian, Gerhard Liedke, presented to the Conference an interpretation of the Bible's creation narrative which is discriminating and illuminating. It contrasts with the uncritical treatment by Lynn White. Liedke points to the clear statement of Gen. 1:29–30 that there is a different distribution of food for men and for animals:

> The animals are to eat "every green plant," that is to say, plants that grow of themselves, which do not have to be cultivated. Man, on the other hand, is assigned corn and the fruits of the trees, that is to say, plants that need cultivation and tending, agriculture. Man does not eat animals; he is a vegetarian. This vegetarianism is not given any metaphysical basis, but represents the ecologically significant avoidance of conflict.[12]

Whenever animals and men dispute over their habitations and food, Liedke concludes, it is man who has the power to decide, for he alone is made in the image of God and has the dominion.

Such was the situation described in prelapsarian Eden, man and nature before the Fall. After the Fall, Adam and Eve and their race experienced disruption, contradiction, and violence as the result of sin. Hence, there was an abrupt change of relationship after the Flood, which was sent by Yahweh because of man's sin. (Noah must have known how to exercise dominion in coaxing and herding all those paired animals into the ark!) When Noah and his family debarked on Mount Ararat, Yahweh effected a "new creation" order. In addition to the same commandment given to Adam—"Be fruitful and multiply and then fill the earth"—a new one was given to Noah, which allowed man to be carnivorous: "Every moving thing that lives shall be food for you," and every beast and bird will have fear and dread of man, the master, for "into your hands they are delivered" (Gen. 9:2–3). Eat animals?—Yes. But destroy them wantonly?—No. Even in this covenant with Noah, there is no *carte blanche* for ruthless domination over nature. The Swiss theologian, Karl Barth, wrote of Noah's race:

> He is already on his way to homicide if he sins in the killing of animals, if he murders an animal. He can only kill it, knowing that it

does not belong to him but to God, and that in killing it he surrenders it to God in order to receive it back from him as something he needs and desires.[13]

We can easily see what happened, however, when the concept of responsible dominion was corrupted by man whose "heart is evil from his youth" (Gen. 8:21). It may be significant that Noah's first reported activity after building an altar to Yahweh was to plant a vineyard. Having permission now to eat meat, he perhaps wanted good wine with his dinner. So the next thing to be written of Noah was that he got drunk (9:21). Just so, the warrant to exercise hegemony over nature proved to be an intoxicating opportunity for human beings. The tradition which eventually was spread by Christianity found a ready counterpart in the human disposition toward acquisitiveness and greed. These materialistic influences were reinforced by another common distortion of the biblical faith, namely, that prosperity and power are "blessings of God," regardless of how the wealth and privilege are acquired. A Bible reader's sharp eye could even sense a subtle bias toward wealth in the very first words describing the land around Eden: "The gold of that land is good" (Gen. 2:12). In any case, the pious implication of faith is clear. Being the crown of creation, man (male and female) is the creature for whom all other creatures exist. The ontological gulf between Adam's race and all other animals—though created on the same day with him—becomes so broad and deep as to be impassable and discontinuous in value before God.

Emphasizing this disjunction between humans and nature, Lynn White employs an idea which, though often expressed, is not self-evidently valid. It is the concept of desacralizing nature according to biblical faith, though he does not use this word. In the animistic religious view of pagans, every tree, spring, stream, hill—indeed, everything—had its own spirit. It was sacralized and worthy of respect, fear, and worship. "By destroying paganism, Christianity made it possible to exploit nature in a mood of indifference to the feelings of natural objects," he writes.[14] Feelings! Cutting a desacralized or deanimated tree was, for Christians, just a way to clear space or get fuel and lumber. Now, it is true that Judaism and Christianity invite worship of the one sovereign, transcendent God, beside whom there are no others. The *shema* is fundamental to faith: "Hear, O Israel, the Lord thy God is one." Divinities of earth and sky and sea, goddesses of fertility and harvest, gods of sacred groves and stones and mountains are simply idols. Idolatry is the epitome of sin. Jews and Christians have remembered the seductions to nature worship in the land of Canaan, in the Roman Empire, and in Europe and America during the ascendancy of Romanticism. But the obverse of monotheistic affirmation is not that the nonhuman components of nature are valueless and devoid of respect. Lynn White might have given more attention to other important passages of the Bible which show how God's good creation, in all its diverse wonder and beauty, is to be respected by men and women because "the earth is the Lord's" (Ps. 24:1). And without being regarded as being animated, sacralized or desacralized, all things in their way can "praise the Lord":

> You sea monsters and all deeps,
> fire and hail, snow and frost,
>   stormy wind fulfilling his command!
> Mountains and all hills,
>   fruit trees and all cedars!
> ....
>   creeping things and flying birds!
>   (Ps. 148: 7–10)

In fairness, we note that White does mention this great psalm, but does not acknowledge that it represents a good number of Old Testament passages expressing—in his words—"the notion of a spiritual democracy of all creatures." However, he pays tribute to the apocryphal hymn of pre-Christian origin, still used in Christian liturgies.[15] It is the *Benedicite*, "Bless the Lord, all works of the Lord." It is a paraphrase and extension of Psalm 148, and was inserted in the Book of Daniel's story of three young Israelites in the fiery furnace. The hymn calls upon all the works of God to praise him: celestial bodies, earthly meteorological phenomena, waters, hills, plants, birds, beasts, men, Israel, priests, and ever-living souls of persons. The spectrum of valued parts and beings of creation is complete. But there is no manifest reason to conclude that this cosmic paean of praise to the Creator so contradicts Gen. 1:26–28 and Christian orthodoxy that it deserves to be labeled heretical.

Paulos Gregorios is forthright in rebutting the idea of Christianity's disdain for nature: "There was no such process as desacralization of nature because . . . not only was the concept of nature as subhuman creation unknown, but also nature was never 'divine,' since it was not God but only a created reality."[16]

No one can reasonably dispute White's cause for anger over the clear fact that ecological deterioration has gone further in the traditionally and nominally Christian Western world than elsewhere, precisely because of the rapid rise of the scientific-technological civilization. Nor can it be denied that many thinkers, Christian and otherwise, have advanced the dualistic view of man and nature, with man having the only intrinsic value and nature at his arbitrary or even capricious disposal. Indeed, the noted Australian biologist and philosopher, Charles Birch, speaking from within, and not against, Christian faith, throws the charge of human-biased dualism precisely at many scientists, holders of "the dominant scientific technological world-view of today." He is equally critical of Christians who have accepted this caricature of the divine intention for creation.

> It is the cosmology of mechanism in which the universe is conceived as a gigantic contrivance grinding on its way relentlessly to an uncertain eternity. Its component parts, be they nebulae, planetary systems, atoms or living organisms are themselves mechanisms. This is the clockwork view of nature . . . with the human being curiously detached from the rest of nature and with a clockwork God outside it. . . .[17]

To alter the figure, one can hope that the obvious peril of nonhuman nature can change it into an alarm clock, to awaken the human race from its fitful sleep to a responsible wakefulness.

If the stark distinction between the biblical idea of dominion and that of the intrinsic value of all creation cannot stand, can there be a fusion of the two concepts? No doubt. As the Conference Report shows, our "cultural context has radically changed since biblical times [when] humanity was confronted with an overpowering nature."[18] Science and technology have reversed the power relations between humanity and other forms of life, mammals and fish especially. More destructive now than the whaler's harpoon and the hunter's rifle are the everspreading habitations and cities, the technically efficient fisheries, and chemically poisoned air, water, and soil. Having dominion, like lords of the earthly manor, humans are not authorized to exercise their right of lordship, willfully raping their environment. Rather, they have a true dominion of trusteeship, care, and prudent use.

Dominion implies ownership. Trusteeship implies a loan, or temporary care. But these alternatives are not set before created humanity with respect to nature. In biblical faith there is only one *Dominus*, one Lord God. Human dominion is derivative from the Creator's. It is secondary, a viceregency, and hence is responsible to God, just as an appointed steward is finally responsible to his master.

Since "the earth is the Lord's," it cannot be possessed by humanity. It is, so to speak, loaned, not owned. The Conference Report declares this: "God entrusts the land to his covenant people, as a loan. This land is not their possession; even strangers have a right to live there. Every seven years the land, too, is to rest (re-creation) and then every fifty years be redistributed and equally shared out. This is a reminder that the earth is not humanity's property and that we are only tenants of it as God's guests."[19]

In a religious view, the same can be said of human life itself. Individual persons do not have full ownership of themselves and thus do not have the right to dispose of their bodies and lives as they choose. This proprietorship seems self-evidently valid within the purview of a humanism which acknowledges no personal and caring God. That the human right of property and other rights are imputed to persons themselves, without condition, is also, in Jeffersonian terms, one of the truths we hold to be self-evident. Democratic societies are built upon such premises. But transcending the immanent democratic society, and the various acknowledged rights of ownership, is the theocratic order in which these rights are seen to be conditional and provisional.

Meanwhile, back at the Garden, discussion continues on how to reconcile and coordinate dominion and stewardship. Two voices can be heard again here: Barth and Gregorios, voices of Western and Eastern theology.

Of the human representative, Adam, Barth writes:

He is not set up as lord over the earth, but as lord on the earth which is already furnished with these creatures. Animals and plants do not belong to him; they and the whole earth belong only to God. But he takes precedence over them. They are provided for his use. They are his "means of life."[20]

Adam—humanity—is preeminent. Of this there can be no doubt. Of no other creature is it, or can it be, said that it bears "the image of God." Does this mean that the Bible, Judaism, and Christianity are mainly anthropocentric? No, they are mainly theocentric. But in a derived and secondary sense, where terrestrial existence is experienced, the faiths are strongly, and without apology, centered on humanity. Lynn White charges that this belief is the root cause of our present ecological disaster. But it is more accurate to say that the root cause is the pervasive human selfishness, which uses this theological insight as a cloak and excuse for ecological pillaging. As the biologist, René Dubos, insists, "we cannot escape an anthropocentric attitude which puts man at the summit of creation while still a part of it."[21] And he argues for "enlightened anthropocentrism."

There is a practical common sense which supports the mandate of ecological stewardship in the name of enlightened anthropocentrism. This is the prudent, thrifty idea that the more of a good thing you can save now, the more will be available in the future. Even the squirrels know this. And insects provide food for the offspring which they will never see. Such good management of the earth's resources is wholly commendable and, indeed, indispensable for the human future. But in the view of Gregorios, it is not quite satisfactory. He writes: "It is wrong to set man's domination of nature over against his stewardship of it. Replacing the concept of domination with the concept of stewardship will not lead us very far, for even in the latter there lies the hidden possibility of the objectification and alienation which are the root causes of the sickness of our civilization."[22] Those Christians who are developing a positive attitude toward conservation can be understood if they opt readily, and even enthusiastically, for the idea of stewardship. It has the virtue of seeming at once practicable, reasonable, and entirely in accord with the biblical teaching that God cares for his created world and man owes primary responsibility to God. The fact that stewardship of nature is consonant with theology does not, however, make it a Christian imperative. It is possibly implicit in the Old Testament, but not explicit. In the New Testament, stewardship clearly refers to human discipleship rather than ecology, as John Passmore has persuasively demonstrated.[23]

The problem is not merely whether humanity uses nonhuman nature for its own livelihood, but how all of nature is to be regarded in itself, in its own intrinsic value. A man may want to have sea-turtle soup and build his house of finest redwood timber; he may like the enjoyable diversions of driving his car at high speed for long distances or of running his snowmobile across white fields where small animals and tender plants are hibernating. Such desires pose ecological questions of a personal kind for people of affluence.

There are questions also for the poor of the world, but they are not just personal choices because the poor, the really destitute, have neither the power nor resources to choose. The poor also need soup and houses, and if such can be made only from endangered species of turtle and tree, they will have to use them. The poor are the "anthropoor" and must take precedence over nature if they have no other available choice but to use the scarce resources.

Concretely, the dilemma faces poor people in various but equally tragic ways. The people of East Africa struggle with two exemplary problems involving trees and elephants. When economic conditions are bad in a land of insufficient minerals, farming, and industry, one source of income is charcoal. Trees, which are relatively scarce, can be cut and half-burned to make charcoal; there is a market for this fuel in treeless desert countries of the Arabian Peninsula not far across the Indian Ocean. Decreasing the quantity of trees exposes the soil to drought and erosion, and thus hastens the process of desertification. So the charcoal business is one of the causes for the southward movement of the great and awful North African desert.

Elephants roam in herds in East Africa, though many still are sacrificed for their ivory and hides. Where hunting has been outlawed the poachers still pursue their search-and-destroy missions. But what shall farmers do when the herds come? A year's work of cultivation, and a year's supply of food for many people, can be destroyed by one day's visit of fifty elephants.

A ruthless and relentless attitude of dominion of the earth conveys to humans the full right to use trees and elephants to secure a basic food supply and the economic necessities.

An attitude of stewardship guiding poor African workers or farmers might still, under duress, give permission to cut the trees and kill the elephants, albeit with a sense of regret. Why regret? Because, some might say, we human beings like to enjoy the sight of trees and benefit by their shady protection from the sun. And who of us is not impressed and thrilled by the spectacle of the huge pachyderms? Moreover, for unremembered generations in India and Sri Lanka the elephants have been trained to be the "heavy machines" for pulling and hauling. In other words, trees and elephants have their uses for men and women.

This is what Gregorios, Birch and others protest against: the objectification of nonhuman nature, and the conferring of value upon it only in human terms. Is there not good reason, a theological reason, why elephants should be protected simply because they are elephants? Do *they* not enjoy being elephants and not merely entertaining human observers or dragging logs?

In the fox hunting country of Virginia, an unknown, seemingly deranged, man shot several purebred horses. No one could suggest his motive. The owners of the stables grieved and were furious, of course. Some told of their affection for the horses. And one man exclaimed, "My God! there are horses around here worth hundreds of thousands of dollars." But no one expressed outrage and sorrow simply because horses, as horses, were shot down.

Illustrative examples like these can be multiplied many times by stories drawn from one's experience or the daily news. For the present discussion of humanity and nature under God they pose two main issues.

If horses, whales, trees, and even rocks have value in themselves, it is called their intrinsic value. They are respectable for no reason of utility or admiration by humanity, according to Claremont philosopher of ecology David R. Griffin. Following the philosophical lead of Alfred North Whitehead, he joined the ecumenical debate by challenging the validity of the biblical and traditional doctrine of creation in Christianity. Again it is the alleged anthropocentrism which is the target of criticism. Griffin sees traditional Christian belief as limiting intrinsic value to humanity alone, as being made in God's image and claiming to have divine commission to rule over all nature. In philosophical terms, this means the discredited dualism of subject and object which is the heritage of René Descartes's influential teaching. Humanity thus enjoys God's conferred autonomy; and all nonhuman or subhuman creation exists only for man's good pleasure. In theological terms, the redemption of humanity is the very purpose of creation.

As shown in the discussion of Lynn White's critique, this belief can have implications of the most far-reaching kind for human civilization and for nature at large. It is a matter of attitudinal conditioning of people rather than of rational reflection by each person upon ancient and authoritative biblical principle. In such a way, one's attitude toward nature's value is shaped just as racism and political inclination are.

A book by Thomas S. Derr of Smith College provoked the critical reaction of Griffin.[24] Derr set forth, as conceptual groundwork for thought on ecological problems, the Christian idea of humanity's unique value and dominion over nature. Griffin understood Derr to be affirming the thought "that human beings should have reverence for other human beings as ends in themselves, as centers of intrinsic value; but that nature should be regarded as devoid of intrinsic value, and hence all intrinsic rights and hence regarded as merely a means to divine and human ends."[25] According to such an exclusive view of human value, nonhuman nature can be regarded not only as useful instrument but as enemy to be conquered. This is not a strange concept in history.

As physicist-theologian William G. Pollard of Oak Ridge National Laboratory acknowledges, "Throughout the course of Western civilization [man] has used his dominion over nature with arrogance and contempt for everything but himself. . . . The tradition of nature as the dark and fearful adversary lies deep in our cultural roots."[26] The eighteenth-century slave trader, and later hymn-writing minister, John Newton, wrote in his memoirs of only the dark horrors of the West African rivers and jungles. The "amazing grace" of God which Newton later experienced was directed entirely to his anguished soul; it had nothing to do with nature. The acknowledged task of nineteenth-century pioneers was "to conquer the wilderness," which meant the destruction of living resources to an extent which we can scarcely imagine today. And now, claim such critics as Griffin, the earth's integrity continues to be threatened by both traditional Christian theology and rapacious materialism, because nature is not respected for its own value and is fair game for whatever exploitation human beings find useful to them. Derr does not say that nature is valueless, but is to be reverenced "only derivatively, as the creation of a good God," and therefore "may not be personified, endowed with selfhood, or otherwise treated on par with man in Biblical religion."[27] Those who, by faith, look at animals and botanical specimens and majestic landscapes as the *opera Domini,* the works of the Lord, can appreciate Derr's testimony. And rather than taking the biblical insight as permission to exploit, they feel its restraint upon them. They do not think that this notion detracts from the value of nature; in fact, it enhances the value because nature is related to God. Christian faith guards against pantheism, common in some religions, wherein God is thought to be contained within creation and be an immanent spirit of nature. The essence of idolatry is to worship the creature rather than the Creator; pantheism is unable to distinguish between them. A pantheist, therefore, might well be a fervid conservationist, going to the extremes of many Hindus and Jains in their diligent avoidance of harming anything that lives. But this degree of sensitivity goes beyond the requirements of a faithful environmental stewardship in Christianity. For here, as has been said, the value imputed to nature by its belonging to God is always conditioned by its relation to the interests of human well-being.

What the devotees of Whiteheadian thought desire, in contrast, is the recognition of nature's intrinsic value, and not just its value in being God's creation and man's environment. The key to understanding this strong belief is the meaning of the word *value.* The word is exceedingly popular today in many realms of discourse, even in some from which until recently it had been excluded, such as science, psychology, and sociology. How is value evaluated in "process" thought? Charles Birch follows Charles Hartshorne by identifying value with feeling:

Only feeling has intrinsic value. If they [pet animals] have no feelings then we should in all logic treat them as we would machines and dispose of them as soon as they become inefficient. There is intrinsic value beyond man. How far down the scale of nature does it extend —to reptiles, frogs, plants, even to plankton? No line can in fact be drawn between man and other animals and plants and cells and even sub-cellular entities. But of course high grade feelings characteristic of conscious man are very different from feelings of so-called lower entities.[28]

To put the idea quite starkly, every living thing has a value independent of human appraisal of it and would have the same value, therefore, if there were no human race. Instead of the traditional "great chain of being," this view sees in everything a "chain of feeling" or a "chain of value." There is no doubt that humanity is at the highest end of the continuum; but down to the lowest level, the smallest link, the elements which constitute all matter, there is no discontinuity. The obvious significance of this philosophy for grasping the relations of God, humanity, and nature is that all creation, under God, is of one consistency. The relative values of all things and living beings must be respected.

It is a common, if deplorable, fact that in countless instances of human history the value of a person has been subordinated to that of an animal or an inert thing. The very basis of human slavery was the belief that this was unobjectionable. It is also an operative principle in all forms of sweatshop labor, some commerce, and much warfare. But this is not what is meant by the advocates of Whiteheadian thought. They fully acknowledge the supreme value of each human being in comparison to all other entities. Humanity is properly situated at the top of the scale, or hierarchy, of all species of living things. Then the scale moves downward according to the approximation to human intelligence and the intensity of feeling. Chimpanzees, apes, and dolphins belong to the upper levels; and research with animals is providing much new data on the basis of which judgments can be made. A human being is not, then, first among equals, but perhaps (we may say) primary among primates and other creatures. Process thinkers would go farther than affirming the intrinsic value of animals in this hierarchy; they speak forthrightly as well of animal rights, analogous to human rights. Opponents of experimental vivisection and persons devoted to the protection of animal pets and wildlife would generally sympathize with the attribution of rights. But this does not mean that those who reject the concept philosophically or theologically are indifferent to the value of animals.

John Passmore is an Australian, like Birch, but this does not result in a common understanding of the humanity-nature relation. Passmore fully disagrees with Birch's consistent emphasis upon the value, or sacredness, of all things in themselves.[29] And the idea of feeling, or sentience, in all things strikes him as being no different in fact from ancient and primitive animism. If Lynn White urged Christianity to find a modern and usable equivalent of animism, somewhat along the lines of the sense which St. Francis of Assisi found in animals, plants, and things, then the Whiteheadian idea might serve. But Passmore will not approve it. Christianity was right in rejecting animistic notions. Trees and rocks are impersonal: "They do not have aims, intentions; they neither love nor hate. We must look elsewhere than to animism if we are in search of a rational foundation for our resistance to ecological destruction."[30] Crude animism, most will agree, is superstition. But process philosophy is a sophisticated pattern of thought which is being appropriated by Christian theologians. They find traditional Christianity mechanistic and thus inadequate as an explanation of perceived reality. Deficient also is materialism, whether scientific, dialectical, or Marxist. Both are deemed to be excessively anthropocentric, even though for very different reasons of belief.

The Conference at M.I.T. was probably the first fully ecumenical meeting in which the ideas of process philosophy and theology were accorded the greatest emphasis. This was evident in the preparatory studies and publications, the main speeches, and the relevant reports from sections. This is to be explained in part by the conference leadership. Metropolitan Paulos Gregorios has taken the lead in interpreting the Eastern Orthodox tradition, emphasizing the belief in the integral unity of humanity and all creation, a belief which has been taught since St. Gregory of Nyssa. Gregorios was moderator of both the planning committee and the world conference; he also presented the main address on the meaning of faith. Professor Birch, as vice-moderator, has worked, written, and spoken extensively within the ecumenical circle. He advances the ideas of Whitehead most ardently, being fully convinced that these can best enable Christians to understand problems of ecology and act upon them. The preparatory papers by Professors John Cobb, Charles Hartshorne, David Griffin, and Schubert Ogden were conspicuous. Paulos Gregorios has clearly acknowledged the affinity between the Cappadocian theology of Eastern Orthodoxy which he professes and the Whiteheadian perspective.[31]

The report of Section II is permeated by such "process" thought and proposes to offer a comprehensive interpretation of Christian doctrine in its terms. This is captured in one lapidary sentence: "The Christian hope sets science and technology in the open-ended process of God's history with his creation."[32] God in his primordial nature is the Creator of all. Yet God also experiences his own changing and evolving history along with his creation. This implies his consequent nature. He moves experimentally toward the perfection of the as-yet-unfinished creation. At the top of the hierarchy of all created entities with their feelings and values is humanity. "All entities from electron to man embody feelings and therefore are of value."[33] Humanity as *homo sapiens* creates science and as *homo faber* develops technology. With full respect for all nonhuman animals and subhuman entities, men and women can freely cooperate with God in the process of becoming complete.

Not only original creation but redemption also is included in this theological project—and this means a profession of the work of Jesus Christ. Highly significant for the relation of humanity and nature to God is the profession of the Incarnation: the union of divine and human in Jesus the Christ. "Since He becomes incarnate not only in the spirit but also in the body of a historical human being, He allows the material world also to share in his saving work."[34] Here the report asserts explicitly the concept which is basic for a distinctly Christian faith. It is more emphatic about Jesus Christ than the American Protestant theologians of Whiteheadian stamp tend to be. In the interpretation of both history and nature there are differing stages of approximation to this christological position. At one level, people who ponder the meaning of the marvelous structures, operations, and relations of everything and every living entity, microcosmic or macrocosmic, feel compelled to acknowledge the order and value of nature, inclusive of humanity, but not to admit any cause or purpose other than a material one.

Moving to the second level, people attribute superior value to the unseen realities of spirit, mind, reason, and purposive direction. In this view, humanity is preeminent, though not necessarily discontinuous from all other entities. The third level is attained when various kinds of "natural theology" can be professed as theory or as belief. These may be: the teaching of pantheism with the divine, sustaining power confined and operative in nature; or the pan*en*theism ("God-in-all") commended by process theologians, who see all things as having their existence within the God who is always becoming; or the teaching that the natural world is God's creation, subject to the preservation and providence of the transcendent God, with moral fulfillment being the principle reason for human existence.

Beyond the natural theologies—pantheistic, panentheistic, deistic or theistic—is the trinitarian faith wherein Jesus Christ is decisive for the full realization of divine intention for both nature and humanity. Scientists who are Christians, or who are sympathetic to Jewish and Christian understanding of the God-nature relation, may see no great intellectual barrier blocking their espousal of some form of natural theology. The constructive interactions of science and faith are readily perceived here. By contrast to natural theologies, the New Testament doctrine of Jesus Christ as the consummator of all creation is hard to conceive, harder to believe, and hardest to explicate. Yet this is what the report affirms as inherent in the faith and theologies of many Christians. It thus goes beyond process theology and becomes consistent with Orthodox, Catholic, and traditional Protestant faith.

If "the Christ" is considered an alternate name for God or transcendent deity, or contrariwise if it is merely the name given to the man Jesus of Nazareth as the prophet who points away from himself to God, then either belief is like a theistic natural theology. In either of these opposite extremes Jesus is only the mediator of a message of the creative and providential power and love of God for the world. Clearly this is not all that the report means. The Christ here is the eternal Son, or Logos, who entered history and became truly human as Jesus; who lived, died, and was raised from death as the bringer of renewed creation. The resurrection of Jesus Christ—not just in the spirit but also in the body—"opens up for the whole creation the possibility of new life out of death."[35]

The keynote of this eschatological belief is freedom. Not only individual persons, not only the church, not only humanity, but all creation is to be set free from its numerous forms of bondage. Such was the astonishing vision of St. Paul, written to fellow believers in Rome; and ever since then it has remained one of the main clues to perceiving the ultimate unity of humanity and nature. Rom. 8:18–23 indicates the coming culmination of the Genesis saga of human creation with the conferred dominion over plants and animals. Just as all creation was "subjected to futility"—the soil corrupted, animals in jeopardy, man in tragic contradiction against God, nature, and himself—so the power of God in Jesus Christ sets creation "free from its bondage to decay" in virtue of "the glorious liberty of the children of God." As nature "fell" with human sin, so will it be "redeemed" or "liberated" by the salvation of humanity in Christ.

What can all this mean in terms other than mystical poetry or mythological fancy? The biblical symbol of consummated freedom is a combination of the bucolic Eden with man's proper urban habitation, Jerusalem. The perfected earthly garden has been depicted visually by artists, from Hieronymous Bosch's *Garden of Delights* to Benjamin West's *The Peaceable Kingdom*. It exhibits all the innocence of an older Walt Disney cartoon. Lions and wolves will be herbivorous; lambs and calves will graze along with them; and the ancient enmity of the serpent toward humans will be rendered innocuous (Isa. 11:6–8; 65:25). Among human beings, conflicts and wars will have ceased, the nations will be healed of strife, evil powers of captivity will be broken, and "death shall be no more" (Rev. 21:4; 22:2; Rom. 8:38–39). One who tries to consider these words and images literally (and thus falsely) will no doubt conclude with Prospero that they are made of "such stuff as dreams are made on." To take them seriously, however, and not literally, they may be translated into terms of our actual experience and realistic hope. The German theologian, Jürgen Moltmann, has struggled profoundly with problems of injustice and oppression within human society and between humanity and nature. He sees a most important idea here.

> Investigations into the ecology of survival have demonstrated, on the sub-human plane, that where competing organisms adapt to one another (*symbiosis*) they have a much better chance of survival than those which continue to conflict with one another in the "struggle for existence.". . . Man will not rediscover the image of God upon the earth through the domination of nature or by the exploitation, in demonic fashion, of natural systems for his own ends. For Christian faith, Christ is "the true man" and "the image of God" upon earth. . . . In the light of Christ's ministry, Gen. 1:28 ought to be completely re-interpreted: no longer "have dominion over the earth" but

"liberate the earth through partnership with it." According to Rom. 8 the enslaved creation is waiting for the "revelation of the freedom of the children of God" through which it, also, is to be liberated.[36]

There is a clear correlation between Christ's life of service to others and our general human vocation to serve God through loving one another and respecting his creation. We speak of "caring" for the earth and of animal "husbandry," personal terms which reflect the voluntary symbiosis we should adopt. In virtue of the resurrection, Christ still lives in a body of men and women, his community, his body on earth. By the Spirit of God he enables this community to be his instrument of freedom and peace in the world. When the world is mentioned in this theological context we are inclined to think of humanity only, but there is very good reason to expand its range of reference to the whole of creation as the object of God's liberating action in Christ.

This kind of theological reasoning shows why Christians cannot satisfactorily discuss ecological concerns within the confines of the Book of Genesis, the Psalms, or other Hebrew Scriptures. Faith in Jesus Christ is not a gentile restatement of the faith of Israel nor a pious decoration and embellishment on the older religion. The debate, described above, about human dominion, domination, and stewardship cannot finally be settled apart from the belief in the purpose and direction of history as illuminated by Christ.

More than anyone else in this century, Pierre Teilhard de Chardin has reminded Christians of this biblical hope and has made it known broadly in intellectual and scientific circles. One of Teilhard's personal friends, a fellow Jesuit and theologian, Henri de Lubac, remembered that the favorite biblical passage cited often by the paleontologist was the eighth chapter of Romans. Teilhard believed that humanity and the world really are moving toward that time of release and freedom, as reality becomes increasingly the spiritual dimension of experience which transforms the meaning of the material. His was a unifying vision of the destiny of creation, drawing into itself elements of diverse belief systems, sciences, and views of history. Teilhard's idea of "the within of things," and of continuing evolutionary becoming, is now seen as having affinity to the view of sentient entities in process philosophy. His espousal and exposition of the doctrine of the cosmic Christ, in whom all things cohere, enabled him to speak for the great christological tradition of Western Catholicism and Eastern Orthodoxy, and especially for the Eucharistic theology which sets forth the sacrament, or holy mystery, as a sign of world transfiguration. Moreover, Teilhard's articulated hope for fulfillment in Christ stretched far beyond present preoccupations with ecclesiastical structures and with ephemeral programs to improve the living conditions of people; this commanded the affirmative support of many Protestant thinkers who fear the drag of two very different weights: churchly introversion and secular humanism. Teilhard was both scientist and contemplative theologian, and he believed he could synthesize biblical eschatology and the empirical science of biological evolution. By extrapolating from the recent century's experience of the human race and earthly change, he foresaw the trajectories of evolution converging toward an eventual consummation of creation. It will be known by humanity as the spiritual and psychic conforming to the truth of Christ. While filling the earth with people, increasing the already vast store of knowledge and skill achieved by intelligence, transforming the world of nature, and appropriating the will of God as perfect love—so humanity is moving with all nature through the process of cosmogenesis to the ultimate Christogenesis.[37]

If hope, rather than species survival, is the more appropriate driving power of human beings, it is expressed in many forward-looking ways. The common activity of long-range planning in commercial enterprises, government, and all kinds of social and cultural institutions is one manifestation of hope rather than despair. Another is the practice of projecting utopias, or at least greatly improved societies. The Marxist goal of a harmonious, classless society, free from avaricious and destructive competition such as capitalism engenders, is utopian. So are objectives of various optimistic ideologies: the liberal Kingdom of God movement, Martin Luther King, Jr.'s "I have a dream" motif, the liberated worlds of freedom movements in the Southern hemisphere, and the One World vision of builders of the United Nations, the Council of Europe, and the New International Economic Order. There are Christians participating in all these endeavors. As individuals they may have single-minded obsessions with the elimination of certain wrongs—racism, economic exploitation, political oppression, arrogant nationalism, ecological peril—or the advancement of particular rights and values—human rights, land reform, economic opportunity, health care, education, world peace. All these just obsessions together constitute the substance of humanity's present striving for the good life which God intends for men, women, and children in a friendly and usable environment. However feasible these good objectives may be in opposition to all the well-known contrary evils of the world, the movements which support them are not so far as some might think from the Christogenesis for which Teilhard hoped. As the subtheme of the World Council's conference described the future hope for humanity in Christ, there should be a society marked by the quality of justice for all people, their responsible participation in main decisions which affect their lives, and the sustainability of their earthly home. Is this not what God wants for humankind and nature, and offers them?

NOTES

1. The ecumenical conference on "Science and Technology for Human Development" was held in Bucharest, June 1974, as a preparation for the 1979 Conference on "Faith, Science and the Future." See *Anticipation,* 19 (November 1974): 35.

2. Barry Commoner, *The Closing Circle* (New York: Alfred A. Knopf, 1971), p. 217.

3. C. H. Waddington, "Values, Life Styles and the Future of the Technological Society," *Anticipation,* 17 (May 1974): 39.

4. Francis Parkman, *The Oregon Trail* (Boston: Little, Brown & Co., 1899), p. 419. In the preface to the 1892 edition, Parkman wrote sadly, but without personal remorse, "The buffalo is gone, and of all his millions, nothing is left but bones."

5. *Only One Earth,* ed. Barbara Ward and René Dubos (New York: W. W. Norton, 1972). The World Council of Churches participated in the conference parallel to the United Nations meeting in Stockholm which involved nongovernmental organizations.

6. Mahinda Palihawadana, "Buddhism and the Scientific Enterprise," *Faith and Science in an Unjust World,* vol. 1 (Philadelphia: Fortress Press, 1980), p. 144. He is professor of Sanskrit in Sri Lanka.

7. Joseph Needham, *Science and Civilization,* II (1954), p. 580; cited by Stanley L. Jaki, *Science and Creation* (New York: Science History Publications, 1974), p. 40.

8. Fouad Zakaria, "The Science-Faith Issue in Islam," *Faith and Science,* vol. 1, p. 129.

9. Ibid.

10. John Passmore, *Man's Responsibility for Nature* (New York: Scribner's, 1974), pp. 13–14.

11. Lynn White, "The Historical Roots of Our Ecological Crisis," *Science*, 155 (March 10, 1967): 1203–7; republished in *Western Man and Environmental Ethics*, ed. Ian G. Barbour (Reading: Addison-Wesley Publishing Co., 1973), pp. 18–30.

12. Gerhard Liedke, "Solidarity in Conflict," *Faith and Science*, vol. 1, pp. 75–76.

13. Karl Barth, *Church Dogmatics, The Doctrine of Creation*, vol. 3, Part 4 (Edinburgh: T. & T. Clark, 1961), p. 355.

14. Lynn White, "Historical Roots."

15. Lynn White, "Continuing the Conversation," *Western Man and Environmental Ethics*, ed. Ian G. Barbour (Reading: Addison-Wesley Publishing Co., 1973), pp. 60–62.

16. Paulos Gregorios, *The Human Presence* (Geneva: World Council of Churches, 1979), p. 27.

17. Charles Birch, "Nature, Humanity and God in Ecological Perspective," *Faith and Science*, vol. 1, p. 64.

18. *Faith and Science*, vol. 2, p. 33.

19. Ibid., p. 31.

20. Karl Barth, *Church Dogmatics*, vol. 3, Part 4, p. 351.

21. René Dubos, "A Theology of the Earth," *Western Man and Environmental Ethics*, ed. Ian G. Barbour, p. 53.

22. Paulos Gregorios, *Human Presence*, p. 29.

23. John Passmore, *Man's Responsibility*, p. 29.

24. Thomas S. Derr, *Ecology and Human Need* (Philadelphia: Westminster Press, 1975). Originally published under the title *Ecology and Human Liberation* (Geneva: World Council of Churches, 1973).

25. David R. Griffin, "Human Liberation and the Reverence for Nature," *Anticipation*, 16 (March 1974): 25.

26. William G. Pollard, "God and His Creation," *This Little Planet*, ed. Michael Hamilton (New York: Scribner's, 1970), p. 67.

27. Thomas S. Derr, *Ecology*, p. 52.

28. Charles Birch, *Confronting the Future* (Ringwood, Australia: Penguin Books, Ltd., 1975), pp. 119–20. The same idea of feeling in all matter is expressed by Charles Hartshorne, "God and Nature," *Anticipation*, 25 (January 1979): 58–63; and by Charles Birch and John B. Cobb, Jr., "God's Love, Ecological Survival and the Responsiveness of Nature," *Anticipation*, 16 (March 1974): 32–34.

29. Passmore, *Man's Responsibility*, pp. 175–76.

30. John Passmore, *Science and Its Critics* (New Brunswick: Rutgers University Press, 1978), p. 62.

31. Paulos Gregorios, *Human Presence,* pp. 46–48.

32. *Faith and Science,* vol. 2, p. 34.

33. Birch and Cobb, Jr., "God's Love," p. 33.

34. *Faith and Science,* vol. 2, p. 31.

35. Ibid.

36. Jürgen Moltmann, "Creation and Redemption," *Creation, Christ and Culture,* ed. Richard W. A. McKinney (Edinburgh: T. & T. Clark, 1976), p. 133.

37. For the rich discussions of Pierre Teilhard de Chardin see especially his basic essay, *The Phenomenon of Man* (New York: Harper's, 1959); *The Future of Man* (New York: Harper and Row, 1964); *Building the Earth* (New York: Avon, 1965); *Christianity and Evolution* (New York: Harcourt Brace Jovanovich, 1971). Also, Bernard Towers, *Evolution, Marxism and Christianity* (London: Garnstone, 1967).

4 | Prometheus Rebounds.../ Genetics, Eugenics, Dysgenics

NOT FIRE, BUT LIFE ITSELF

Just as children identify themselves with real or legendary heroes, so human beings look to a number of prototype figures. These, too, are either mythical or historical. They are paragons of certain qualities or symbols of particular abilities in which people take pride. Gautama Buddha is humanity's ideal of one who suppresses desires and appetites and finds reality in sustained contemplation. Confucius is the person of culture, who with equanimity avoids extremes, living a disciplined, dignified life. Job is Everyman, who knows acute deprivation and suffering, but whose confidence in God's goodness is so unshakable that he remains uncrushed by assorted evils. Jesus is the one who perfectly expresses altruistic, self-sacrificing love by his cruel death, but who overcomes that death by God's power of renewed life. Renunciation, balance, trust despite suffering, and new life out of costly love are, to varying tastes and faiths, commendable aspects of human life.

None of these four figures, however important for giving meaning to millions of people's lives, exalts the initiative and power of human beings themselves. Passivity, moderation, trust, love, and hope are personified by them. None can be the symbol of man's technological and scientific advance. This is why writers on science often turn to Greek mythology, where creatures inspire admiration, not because they obey or trust the gods, but because they contend against them. Two of the Titans are often adduced as the "patron saints" of modern science.

One is Atlas, who was required by Zeus to hold up the heavens on his powerful arms and shoulders. Robert Heilbroner thinks of Atlas as the most appropriate type of humanity today. By "bearing with endless perseverance the weight of the heavens in his hands," he shows the "fortitude and will" needed by humanity to survive today.[1] Therefore, space rockets, not so strangely, are named Titan and Atlas.

More frequently thought of today, however, is his brother Prometheus. The name means "foresight." On behalf of mankind, he stole the creative fire from Zeus, the source of energy indispensable to civilization. For this daring theft, according to Hesiod and Aeschylus, Zeus created Pandora and sent her to earth with her jar (not box) of many evils to punish the rebels. Then Prometheus was bound by chains to a rock in the sea, tormented by a ravenous carnivorous eagle, until Heracles unbound him. Released, Prometheus could build up human technological civilization, making way for invention of metallurgy and tools, civil engineering, the uses of physics, chemistry, biomedical knowledge, and eventually commercial television.

In our day, Prometheus, unbound, has rebounded with unprecedented vigor and power. And as in defiance of the eagle sent from Zeus, it was under an eagle's sign that he victoriously held up, not the captured fire, but life itself. One day in April 1953, in Cambridge, England, in a pub named The Eagle, microbiologist Francis Crick said aloud, "We have found the secret of life." That morning, he and the young American, James D. Watson, with their colleague, Maurice Wilkins, knew at last the structure and genetic function of the DNA molecule. The knowledge "had emerged from the shadow of billions of years, absolute and simple, and it was seen and understood for the first time. Twenty angstrom units in diameter, seventy-nine billionths of an inch."[2] Once the operative code of the two twisting strands of living matter in the large molecule of deoxyribonucleic acid had been identified, the science of molecular biology advanced more rapidly than any other branch of science has ever done.

If modern scientific work might be likened to a long working day, now is the rush hour of the life sciences. The coalescence of sciences is noted in Crick's definition of molecular biology: "the chemical physics of biology."[3]

For centuries, and especially during the one just past, human wit, knowledge, skill, and daring have been reshaping the environment. Not only the immediate surroundings of human habitation, but actually the whole earthy and watery face of the planet has been affected. For better or worse? That is not now the question. What needs emphasis is the new fact: that Promethean man can deliberately change the nature of human beings and other kinds of organisms and organic life. It is to be noticed, then, that the popular idea of "the eighth day of creation" implies a creative act following the seventh primordial day on which God himself had to rest. Promethean man takes over where Yahweh leaves off in this mixing of Jewish and Greek stories. Jewish and Christian Scriptures had just a slight affinity for some gods of the Greek pantheon, although their monotheism could never allow them to call these gods God. Yet, Wisdom (Pallas Athene) and Healing (Asclepius) represented most agreeable aspects of life. Prometheus, by contrast, has never been welcome in synagogue or church. The essence of sin is to set oneself against God, or to try to preempt his divine power. Adam and Eve were held to be responsible for this worst of all sinful pretensions: wanting to eat the fruit of the Tree of Life, to be "like God, knowing good and evil." Their early descendants, who built the first cities and the great ziggurat called the Tower of Babel, were the would-be biblical counterparts of Prometheus. But the great prophets declared that Yahweh laughed at these human conceits and put them down by his acts of judgment. Before God, man must know his place. The pot must not challenge the potter.

This characteristic belief became a deeply imbedded attitude of serious Christians over the centuries: so in their own view the great and pious scientists of the early modern age were not eating forbidden fruit, or stealing fire, but "thinking God's thoughts after him." They said they were only discovering little by little some of the vast inexhaustible store of wonderful truth which God the Creator had locked into nature in all its forms. That view is still a satisfying one for many and, indeed, required by their theology. In respect to living tissue, especially the higher organisms and human life, this respectful restraint has been maintained as a matter of religious belief and obligation. In debate with materialist biologists who dared to have Promethean ambitions, Christian apologists could usually declare the final rebuttal: "You will never create life or know its originating mystery; God alone knows that." This argument had a certain cogency before 1953. Does it have any now? The answer is arguable.

Biologists have not "created" life in the sense of growing living organisms from inert matter. They are neither likely, nor intending, to do so. But the "secret of life" is not found in the shaping of organisms; it is in the transition from cells which have no nuclei (prokaryotes) to those which do (eukaryotes), and in the chemical mechanisms by which cells reproduce themselves. The distinction between the former type, which include only the bacteria and blue-green algae, and all other kinds of living cells is a gap far wider than, say, the separation of plants and animals.[4] Scientists within only two decades have been learning to theorize, with supporting evidence of clearly detailed fossilized cells, how certain chemical conditions on the earth some 3.5 billion years past could have brought the nonnucleic living cells into existence. They can even, with some success, set up the same conditions in a laboratory and illustrate (if not demonstrate) how four of the twenty amino acids requisite to the forming of protein could have come together. Moreover, they have closed the gap between the two kinds of cells, bacteria and viruses, and provided the conditions for their reproduction to take place. The newspaper headings have called this laboratory experiment "creating life," which it is not—not yet. But some scientists do not hesitate to predict even creation of living tissue will come in the future.

The French biologist, François Jacob, expresses the thinking of many colleagues when he rejects the traditional notion that the task of the life sciences is just to reveal what is found or happening naturally in nature. Of biology he writes, "It is no longer seeking for truths. It is building its own truth."[5] Prometheus in a white coat! First to be rejected is the idea that behind or underlying all natural phenomena there is a causative divine mind, will, or purpose, since the only recognized principle of life is the obvious urge to reproduce. Repeatedly, Jacob insists upon this negation of any metaphysical directing influence upon life processes. Second, in opposition to philosophical naturalism, the idea of a self-contained and self-preserving natural order is sloughed off, like a snakeskin which no longer fits. Without as yet "creating" life, man thus is able to "take life in his hands" and manipulate it as he will and can. This implies the idea that the human species is not as well developed as it might be. The evolutionary process has not run its course; it is now being appropriated and boosted by *homo sapiens* himself. And *homo faber suipsius,* man maker of himself, devises not only tools and techniques but modifies the bodies of humans as such. In 1968 scientist Robert L. Sinsheimer of the University of California observed, as others have since:

> For the first time in all time a living creature understands its origins and can undertake to design its future. Even in the ancient myths man was constrained by his essence. He could not rise above his nature to chart his destiny. Today we can envision that chance—and its dark component of awesome choice and responsibility. . . . We can be the agent of transition to a wholly new path of evolution. This is a cosmic event.[6]

In light of the previous discussion of human dominion over nature—as stewardship rather than ruthless domination—is it not possible that the modern Prometheus, M.D., Ph.D., acts within the moral province of biblical faith? Why should anyone who, for religious reasons, disagrees with Jacob's first premise of rejecting divine causation also have to object to the biologist's modifications of life, and especially of human life? Those who assert that it is "unnatural," and thus contrary to God's will, to attempt genetic interventions in human beings must be able to show why this is less "unnatural" than artificially producing hybrid corn, heavier cattle, or antipolio vaccines. As is often argued, all medicinal and surgical therapy is highly unnatural. So are most of the activities which constitute technology and cultures. The myth of human naturalness, so appealing to many pious and romantic people, ultimately yields the figure of the noble but naked savage, hunting and gathering. If this reduces to absurdity the abhorrence of doing anything "which is against nature," it calls for a much more carefully nuanced definition of what is natural and, as such, immutable.

No, the preferred concept of dominion as stewardship does not prohibit the achievement of countless "unnatural" changes in the ways and commodities of human existence. But genetic science now forces an answer to the question: To what extent may, or should, the bodies and minds of human beings be modified by the fast emerging techniques of intervention, engineering, and therapy of one's genes? Asking this question the philosopher of biology and ethics, Hans Jonas, comments without answering:

> This has become a theoretical possibility with the advent of molecular biology and its understanding of genetic programming; and it has

been *rendered morally possible by the metaphysical neutralizing of man.* . . . Since the same evolutionary doctrine of which genetics is a cornerstone has deprived us of a valid image of man, the actual techniques, when they are ready, may find us strangely unready for their responsible use.[7]

This is the primary cause of concern to people of moral and religious sensitivity: Have human beings now been metaphysically neutralized? The cleavage of belief between those holding opposite views of human identity and dignity goes deepest on this issue.

DOES THE END JUSTIFY THE GENES?

The sudden revolution in genetic science has had a good press: perhaps too good. Many articles, books, and television shows present the potential blessings and curses of the new ability to manipulate and engineer the nucleotides in DNA molecules, causing changes which might never happen naturally. Technical literature is popularized, and popular versions are in turn reduced to the commonplaces of mass media. Of course it is desirable for people to know they are in the midst of this revolution. But the very simplicity of presentation gives the false and dangerous illusion to multitudes that since everything about "the secret of life" has been disclosed, everything is now possible. This is the inclination of the masses who have been taught to place complete, unquestioning confidence in scientific technology. The best example may be the idea of human cloning: growing from some scraps of tissue a human being who would be genetically identical to the one from whom the tissue was taken. While the theory is well-known, the likelihood of achievement is more remote than some other notions of science fiction. Technical problems are too formidable to allow scientists any hope of cloning humans.

Another example of premature expectation lies in an assumed understanding of the way the genetic information coded by DNA molecules actually controls the process which produces every different kind of cell, tissue, and organ in the body. Against such popular credulity the medical scientist and essayist Lewis Thomas confesses:

The only solid piece of scientific truth about which I feel totally confident is that we are profoundly ignorant about nature. Indeed, I regard this as the major discovery of the past hundred years in biology.[8]

And on the proliferation and differentiation of cells in the human embryo which combine to form the cerebral cortex, he adds, "No one has the ghost of an idea how this works, and nothing else in life can ever be so puzzling."[9]

As we who are not biologists discuss recent advances and fantastic prospects in genetic science, we can avoid the illusions of both fear and undue expectancy by heeding the sober cautions of those who are experts.

EUGENE AND EUGENIA

A baby is about to be born. Nine months of a woman's distress, inconvenience, mixed emotions, pleasant expectation and joy will end in a period of painful anguish and incomparable satisfaction of cuddling the newborn girl or boy to her breast.

Will the baby be perfect? Physically without blemish? Mentally normal? Capable of a good, happy, and useful life? These are the inevitable questions of parents, relatives, attending midwives, doctors, and nurses. They are the properly human questions. Whether boy or girl, will Eugene or Eugenia be "well-born"?

At the level of minimal genetic concern, however, there is only one question: will this new specimen of the human animal reproduce itself without causing damage to its progeny? Will it help the species survive?

The two kinds of questions, personal and impersonal, are not unrelated. A "perfect" baby promises a good life; a healthy specimen contributes to human survival in the aeons of struggle against, say, the insects.

Many years before our understanding of the DNA molecule was given its new twist, geneticists were speculating and planning. They speculated on the prospect of a humanity free from myriad congenital defects. They planned ways to achieve that goal. Who could dispute the desirability of their intention? They would eliminate from the genetic stream impurities that caused mental impairment, physical malformations, susceptibility to diseases, and inability to thrive in certain climates and environments. This would mean weeding out those undesirable tares in the human garden which clearly manifest such disabilities. It would also require detection of dangerous genetic cargo being carried by apparently healthy people, who unknowingly might pass on defects to their children and grandchildren.

Recognizing the common truth that "people don't know what's best for them," eugenic theorists noted that strong social pressures and even governmental enforcement would be required. Those who are mentally retarded, psychopathically incorrigible, or physically deformed since birth would have to be first, identified, second, discouraged from reproducing, and third, in hard cases of resistance, prevented by sterilization from perpetuating their deleterious genes. According to this direction of thought, genetic engineering would be transposed from individual cases to become a vast social engineering project. It would change and presumably improve the whole population of a nation and, eventually, the world. Such has been the theory.

Just to think of the kind of totalitarian state which would be required to impose this program of human improvement makes people shudder. A realistic preview of it was provided by Nazi Germany's effort to create the "perfect" Aryan master race. There is no reason to think that Germans could have a monopoly on such atrocities as resulted from Nazi eugenic laws which led to forced sterilization and extermination of thousands. The same theories of genetic inferiority were once used to justify black slavery and social repression in America. And over the period of the past fifty years thousands of persons, mainly of ethnic minorities, were subjected to unknowing or involuntary sterilization, often upon orders of the courts. Though strongly contested today on moral grounds, sterilization is still advocated by some as a way to prevent degeneracy and to economize on public welfare funds.

Does this grim objection to eugenic programming as a totalitarian assault on liberty and life end the discussion? No, there is more to be said.

POLLUTING THE GENE POOL?

There is an ambiguity which for better or worse belongs to the medical profession as well as to the science of genetics. This is the unwelcome fact that the future health of the human race is not guaranteed, but threatened by the prodigious progress of physicians, surgeons, and pharmacologists in healing the sick and extending their lives. Although many people no doubt assume that the future health and wellbeing of the race are in direct proportion to the extensive and effective provision of health care, this is not necessarily true. It is easy to understand why. This optimistic faith is held only at the cost of disregarding the multiple and changing causes of poor health. If genetic diseases can be reduced significantly, and if effective health care be provided for all persons, it will still be necessary to overcome the perils of unhealthful living habits, infectious and chemically dangerous environment, and the spread of chronic degenerative diseases among the increasingly numerous old people. But just now our concern is confined to the genetic dimension of human health.

A pious Christian unadulterated by modern scientific knowledge may say, "God made us as we are," and think no further about the causes of human varieties and ills. Depending upon his religious faith a geneticist may or may not give God the credit for color of eyes and hair and skin, native intelligence, or susceptibility to certain diseases. But he understands rather well now that variations in the genes can account for the transmission of any one of the forty thousand or more variable characteristics of a human being. Some of these are deleterious to both the individual and to larger numbers of persons in succeeding generations.

The phenotype of an individual includes the composite of genes and is unique. When a man and woman join their germ cells in the process of procreation, a rather predictable blending of chromosomes takes place in the progeny. But this is no simple phenomenon, with each child receiving the same proportion and kind of genes from each parent. Because of chemical actions describable but not fully understood, new changes arise in each human being. The random recombination of genes in procreation determines the distinctive characteristics of each individual, both physical and mental. Also, mutations are caused by certain external chemical action, radioactive radiation, or spontaneity. There are inconceivably minute changes of nucleotides in the hundred thousand or more genes in a human cell, and these are responsible for modifications in people which are neither slight nor harmless. Physical malformation, mental retardation, and defenselessness against diseases are the common and negative manifestations.

Geneticists speak confidently of procedures to alter the phenotype of a person so as to ward off particular disabilities and diseases. These include myopia, diabetes, cystic fibrosis, and hemophilia. Until these methods are practically applied, however, the art of medicine enables persons to stay alive for long years while bearing such congenital illness. By such care, medical science is making it possible for millions of people to produce children and enjoy parenthood, who in former generations would not have survived to marriageable maturity. Thus the mutant and impairing genes are passed on to new generations, perpetuating and spreading the inclinations to disease and disability.

People are at last becoming alarmed about the pollution of natural resources caused by a technological and wasteful consumers' economy. Breathing the air of some cities is actually fatal. Lakes and rivers have become vast sewers. Soil, water, and air are jeopardized on a global scale. And people are frightened. But is there not also a biological, or more precisely genetic, pollution which threatens the human race? Are we literally degenerating, being the victims of an uncontrolled process of dysgenics?

"Every time we prolong a life or cure an infectious disease or take care of a mutant," wrote biologist Dr. Paul D. Saltman in 1967, "we are adding to a burden in this society. . . . The consequences of a few pennies of DDT sprayed in a village in Africa to eradicate malaria manifests itself twenty years later in starvation of the increased population."[10] The arts of healing are a wonderful boon as are the methods of disease prevention, but for the human race as a whole the care and healing of persons of certain genotypes may ultimately bring much misery in the years to come. Dr. Theodosius Dobzhansky popularized the plausible but melancholy idea that in future generations the taking of insulin—soon artificially available—will be as widespread and commonplace for endemic diabetes as the use of aspirin for colds and headaches today. The late Hermann J. Muller, of Indiana University, geneticist and Nobel Laureate, became so pessimistic about this trend that his warnings have been called "genetic apocalypse."

If we were to concede the probabilities described by genticists, we would confront a baffling ethical problem. It seems unexceptionable to assert that the health and well-being of humanity should be sustained by all means. But is it possible in any society to secure these benefits for some individuals without causing deprivation to others? It may be true, in Jeffersonian terms, that each one has an inalienable right to life, liberty, and the pursuit of happiness. But if happiness, liberty, and life include, as many believe, the right to marriage and the spawning of children, then these rights will be purchased by some persons at the painful price to society of the poor health and distress of their many descendants. Environmental spoliation and destruction are due to the disregard of one generation for the coming ones. Present satisfaction of desires and physical cravings depends upon the production of thousands of machines, factories, and industries. A spendthrift generation, wasting resources on useless wars, for example, bequeaths massive debts to children and grandchildren. Likewise, it is ironic, unintentional, and paradoxical that the present quest for all-around better health will pollute the genetic pool of the race.

Can the pool be cleansed? And is the coming stage of critical pollution really so imminent? Scientists disagree among themselves about the urgency of this threat. While many specialists are deeply concerned about the danger to babies yet to be conceived and born, most people are ignorant of the issue and too busy to think about it if they did know and understand. Despite the indifference and ignorance, this is a matter of personal gravity for far more people than we may realize. In fact, relatively few families are unaffected by some genetic aberrations. And beyond one's personal involvement in a known family problem, every responsible person should have an informed opinion on the ethical issues involved.

CAN ANYTHING BE DONE?

Yes, something can be done. Practical proposals are being made. Reproduction can be prevented by contraception or sterilization. Genetically impaired progeny can be diagnosed before birth and their lives terminated prematurely by abortion. The natural desires for parenthood can be at least partially satisfied by adoption, even though adoptive parents now have less choice among children than formerly. The advocates of planned eugenics offer another alternative: when a husband is known to have genes which are likely to impair a child, his wife can be impregnated with the sperm of another man through the simple procedure of artificial insemination. Looking to the future, as the technique for direct intervention in the genes becomes perfected, it will be feasible to modify the genetic composition of a very young human embryo and correct its defects at the outset of life. These things *can* be done. But *should* they be done? Such is the question of ethics put before each option.

One of the clichés of modern folklore is the answer given by the alpinist to the question, "Why do you climb to that mountain peak?" Drawing upon his pipe and directing his gray-blue eyes to the distant snows, he calmly replies, "Because it's there."

It is easy to liken every researcher in every branch of science to that alpinist. He attacks the problem because it is there, challenging all of his mental ability. But are there scientific cliffs and peaks which are better left unclimbed? To be specific about genetics, are there not both calculated risks and incalculable ones with respect to basic human values? Should not the incalculable ones be either assumed with utmost caution and trepidation, or else avoided entirely? Sometimes it may be better to yield to fear and prudence than to try to outdo Prometheus. This was the kind of decision made by eighteen German physicists headed by Dr. Carl Friedrich von Weizsäcker, when they took their historic stand against building an atomic bomb.

Of comparable significance was the unprecedented position taken in 1974 by American microbiologists to impose upon themselves a moratorium on research using recombinant DNA. They were poised to venture boldly into the unknown future of splicing genes and developing new strains of bacteria and viruses, which conceivably could cause irrepressible epidemic diseases. They looked to the Alpine slopes, so to speak, and said, "Not yet." Instead, they gathered at Asilomar on the coast of California and deliberated on the socially and ethically acceptable uses of the radically new technique of altering the gene structure of living organisms, including humans. Research did not resume until certain safeguards had been agreed upon by the scientists and by such appropriate public agencies as the National Institutes of Health. The accepted guidelines of 1976 left open enough loopholes to keep researchers busy in their laboratories, looking for multiple uses of genetic engineering for agriculture, industry, pharmacology, and medicine. All federal restrictions were finally lifted in January 1980, when the safety factors and laboratory controls had been shown to be satisfactory.[11] Hardly a week now passes when the news media do not report some important new discovery or development in the field of microbiology and genetics.

Scientists are not at all like the mad geniuses of horror films and sci-fi fiction. But there is division in their ranks as to the capability of all scientists to make responsible decisions which affect social ethics and human welfare. To ask about their competence in ethics presupposes their understanding of human nature and life itself. By their own expressions, many identify themselves with the large number of people who reject belief in the spiritual or metaphysical dimension of human identity. They see human intelligence and character as being caused only by the maximal evolution of the cerebral cortex and the adaptive ability to assimilate concepts and values from the cultural environment which, inexplicably, has developed through the centuries. Scientists who are thus committed to a philosophy of scientific materialism may or may not always think and act in consistency with their world view. It is respectful, not condescending, to observe that they, too, are civilized, decent, and moral. They share an intention for honoring the dignity of life, promoting individual health and a good society. But should they *alone* be entrusted with decisions and policymaking about research and technology which affect some of the deepest values of human life? Or, cannot other persons of different philosophies, based upon religious sources of understanding, participate?

Questions about the ethical acceptability of the various modes of reproduction control in the interests of genetic improvement are not all of the same order. Contraception, sterilization, abortion, and artificial insemination are well established techniques with predictable consequences, however sharply divided people may be over their moral legitimacy. But the proposed procedures of genetic intervention by transferring cell nuclei, splicing genes, and using recombinant DNA technology on the human body are still in the realm of both moral and pragmatic uncertainty.

The World Council of Churches conference at M.I.T. took cognizance of the truly beneficial consequences and possibilities of genetic engineering for treating diabetes, sickle-cell anemia, and hemophilia.[12] Also, the agricultural benefits appear to be nearly limitless when new strains of bacteria are developed to provide fertilizers. Even so, the conference warned against the danger of our drifting into a tacit belief in genetic determinism and of the disposition to allow scientists to do whatever they wish with individual human genotypes. Some who speak with Christian conscience urge others not to worry about these matters. The inevitability of scientific discovery is obvious, however vigorous may be objections raised against some forms of it. Moreover, the biblical warrant for human dominion over earth, animals, and environment must include the use of eugenics as well, they argue.

Does Genesis, then, imply an unconditional legitimation of genetics? It is arguable. Among those who take the biblical story of Adam's commission to have dominion seriously, rather than merely literally, there is division of thought. It is asserted that the hegemony of man over environment and animals is conditioned and limited only by considerations of human well-being. As seen above, this is precisely the core of the theological issue in today's ecological crisis. But the dominion of the human race over itself even to the point of participating in its own further evolution may not be absolute and unconditional. Unless God's reality be denied, or human dependence upon him and a sense of responsibility be considered otiose, the questions of what can be done and what should be done cannot have one and the same answer. Scientists, politicians, or persons of much power do indeed presume to play God whenever they believe themselves to be competent to make ultimate and irrevocable decisions which would determine the genetic future of society. Such Promethean arrogance repudiates and usurps the sovereignty of God. Or, to reduce the discussion from the loftiness of these affirmations of faith in God, we may ask if there are not some basic, categorical, or transcendent human values which militate against some programs of positive eugenics and risky genetic engineering. The intrinsic, inviolable worth of each person, or developing person, is one such acknowledged value. The given reality of marriage and family, though much violated and challenged today, is another.

As research pushes forward on many fronts in the life sciences, and as the public becomes more intelligently aware of the possible implications of what is being done, the problem of imposing or exercising restraint in biological experimentation and genetic planning becomes increasingly acute. We can be sure that the problem will increase in complexity and urgency, defying consensus on how to deal with it.

EUGENIC PROGRAMS: VOLUNTARY OR COERCED?

The ethical issues of the uses of emerging scientific knowledge are drawn most sharply by the proposals which are most extreme. That is why it seems unavoidable in any discussion of the ethics of genetics to give attention to the ideas of the late Hermann J. Muller. Not only did he achieve the highest recognition in genetic research but he was also a most imaginative, articulate, and passionate advocate of positive or planned eugenics. In the same order of fervid enthusiasm as Billy Graham, he was an evangelist, not for the *euangelion* but for *eugenesis*. His name does not stand alone in this campaign. Sir Julian Huxley and J. B. S. Haldane in England, Jean Rostand in France, and Frederick Osborn in America have shared his hope that the human race may eventually be remade through eugenic planing.

Reflecting upon their research and knowledge, eugenicists concluded that *homo sapiens* can be modified in the direction of superior physical and mental traits. Obviously, sweet corn and beef cattle have been improved by scientific breeding. In effect, it is simply a matter of breeding out and breeding in, so that undesirable genotypes may become extinct and desirable ones flourish. All that stands in the way of the deliberate improvement of the human stock are the existing laws (or lack of them) and public opinion. A great many people are not persuaded that human beings can be manipulated and controlled in the same way as beef cattle. Taking exception to these proposals of his colleagues on the scientific Olympus, Sir P. B. Medawar expressed his dissent:

> The practices of stockbreeders can therefore no longer be used to support the argument that a policy of positive eugenics is applicable in principle to human beings in a society respecting the rights of individuals. The genetical manufacture of supermen by a policy of cross-breeding between two or more parental stocks is unacceptable today, and the idea that it might one day become acceptable is unacceptable also.[13]

There are no blocks of public opinion against negative eugenics among those who understand the matter. This is also called preventive eugenics. Here the freedom and integrity of persons are respected and are not subjected to coercion. Genetic counseling services are the key to success. Just as a young man or woman on the threshold of marriage are required by law to have tests for venereal disease—which is a coercive measure—so they can voluntarily agree in consultation with specialists to have their individual and family genotypes explored and described. When advised that they are carriers of debilitating genes that, according to Mendelian principles, can render their children physically or mentally defective, they have the right to accept or reject the counsel to abstain from producing their children by normal intercourse. Adoption, artificial insemination, or even abstention from marriage are among their options. But they are free options, the moral decisions being borne by the two people concerned. In the United States this kind of important premarital counseling has made a relatively small beginning. If the millions of men and women who plan to be married soon begin to take advantage of such services, the number of genetic specialists who can render them must be vastly increased. Also, as knowledge of the subject comes to be publicly understood, there will doubtless be pressures upon legislators to require by law the testing of men and women before marriage licenses may be issued. This could not prevent procreation outside of marriage —and the present revolution in sexual mores and morals may make extramarital procreation seem even more acceptable than it is in the view of libertarians. Nevertheless, it would mark the strong tendency for the society to move from the present option of voluntary negative eugenics to the stage of coerced negative eugenics and thence to programmed or positive eugenics. During this projected time, if such be the movement of thought and attitude, the geneticists themselves will surely keep moving toward deeper and more detailed knowledge in their field with a consequent increase in skills and powers of intervention and manipulation.

This movement is precisely what those who identify themselves with Muller and Huxley desire. Underlying the approach to positive eugenics is the supposition that the geneticists will in time be authorized by society to plan and execute the breeding of a superior kind of human strain. It would seem from Muller's description of a genetically improved race that this is something which can be done now, if the scientists were given ample opportunity to exercise their knowledge and techniques. Vast amounts of data regarding the genotypes of persons in successive generations would have to be stored in computers, and this is now quite feasible. Procreation could be effected naturally through the sexual union of "certified" husband and wife (assuming the continuance of monogamous marriage which is at least one-at-a-time), but first the selection of spouses would have to be made with the guidance of the counselors. Otherwise, if couples wanted to marry for such traditionally respected reasons as love or money, there would be available the technique of artificial insemination using selected sperm.

It has been known for three decades, thanks to the research of Dr. Hudson Hoagland, that human spermatozoa can be kept, like orange juice, in the deepest of freezes until carefully thawed and used for the fertilizing of ova. This technique even allows the spermatogonia, which produce the spermatozoa, to be frozen and then resume their proper purpose. Technically considered, there is no problem in perfecting this method still further, wrote Muller years ago. Only what he impatiently called the "superstition" of the public stands in the way.[14] Since he wrote of this, the banking and withdrawing of frozen sperm has become a reality. There is actually an extensive amount of artificial insemination being practiced today with the frozen sperm of both known and unknown men. A kind of natural repugnance to the very idea of it, whether for moral, psychological or aesthetic reasons, has been losing its restraining power. Religious ethical opinion is clearly divided over its legitimacy. Catholic moralists and others of conservative view equate the practice with adultery if the sperm be that of a man other than the husband. Probably there is no more likelihood of Christian churches reaching a near concensus on this than on the comparable issues of contraception and abortion (see pp. 137ff.).

Considered only in practical judgment, artificial insemination in America is largely unplanned and not scientifically monitored. Muller would have the practice regularized. Donations would be received by sperm banks from men of acknowledged superiority in intelligence, talent, physical strength, and congenial and cooperative disposition. The greater the quantity of sperm from such preferred "fathers," the better for the coming society. Sperm of outstanding males would be kept in the frozen banks for one or two decades before use—not for aging, as with wine, since fresh sperm is best, but in order to allow time for the donor to pass from the earthly scene. This delay of two decades or more would eliminate all problems of real or imagined personal relations with the woman who would bear the child. Also, the time would permit the geneticist to make a careful selection of the type of sperm most appropriate for a certain woman.

Assuming the acceptance of so rational a scheme, Muller held extravagant hopes for humanity in future generations. Being sensitive to humanistic and cultural values, he saw the emergent ideal genotype. Intelligence, health, and cooperativeness would be the primary characteristics, along with such ideal qualities as St. Paul once attributed to the intervention of the Holy Spirit: love, joy, peace, . . . (Gal. 5:22). Muller also saw no reason why husbands whose wives had been impregnated with the sperm of geniuses and Nobel Laureates would not be genuinely proud of their foster children and as affectionate toward them as to their own seed. Moreover, in his boundless optimism about human character, Muller believed that where the coupling of man and wife with procreative results still goes on, undirected and unaided by science, parents of excellent genetic endowment could produce large numbers of children and give them for adoption to foster parents, thus proving, in his words, that they are "socially minded."

It is no wonder that Theodosius Dobzhansky expressed impatience and disdain for those whom he styled "otherwise outstanding scientists."[15] Muller's gospel of eugenic planning is certainly vulnerable to both waggish ridicule (for example, "The First National Sperm Bank of Bloomington") and serious criticism by other scientists, sociologists, and ethicists. One vigorous ethical critique has its source in the biblical concept of human creation and the complementarity of man and woman. This is the objection to Muller's kind of thinking which was launched by Professor Paul Ramsey, an influential theological ethicist of Princeton University. Having devoted a prodigious amount of study to the life sciences, law, and medicine, Ramsey trenchantly charges Muller with failing to discern or respect the distinction between unitive love and procreative love, and their inseparable connection as well.[16] The very humanness of man and woman is outraged if they are treated as intelligent animals. Traditional Roman Catholic concepts of marriage and procreation have centered too emphatically on the procreative purpose of unitive love as sexually expressed, and this has diminished the integrity of unitive love. But the positivistic geneticists at the other extreme would rend asunder these two types of love. The "genetic apocalypse" of degeneration could not be worse than the horrors of dehumanized modes of procreation which Muller's ideas, implemented by political legislation and controls, would produce.

EUGENICS IN A HURRY

The main ethical arguments against positive eugenic planning, other than by mere counseling, are that it would do violence to the essential meaning which human beings find in the conjoining of the unitive and procreative goods in sexual union; also that it would jeopardize the integrity of persons with free and responsible moral choice. This latter condition would be so, inasmuch as no eugenic program of wide effect could succeed without strong pressures being brought to bear upon people who love freedom and hate coercion.

We thus return to the matter of private decision and the sense of social obligation with respect to one's role in the genetic improvement of the race. If, in terms of negative eugenics, people are made aware of having defective genes, they must decide whether to follow one of the ways by which fertilization can be prevented. If, for reasons of positive eugenics, a couple is advised that the sperm of some donor will assure a normal or superior genotype in the offspring of the wife, they must be helped to know the facts and the serious ethical considerations before making a decision. In either case, they should be well aware of the social implications of their action beyond the private meaning. "The basic factor," wrote Dobzhansky, "is the people's willingness to give in their private lives some consideration to the good of the supra-individual units, starting with their own families and moving to mankind as a whole."[17] And Ramsey, departing from his well-grounded polemics against Muller, agrees that we should encourage "an ethics of genetic duty," whereby the multiple issues of procreation will be resolved not only according to personal desires but also for the sake of coming generations.[18]

These judgments are calm, reasonable, and ethically consistent. But is there *time* allowed to mankind for eugenics to be made effectual by the reasonable voluntarism of socially responsible people? Much of the foregoing discussion has been written as though time were not a factor, and a most urgent one at that. The good effects of any voluntary eugenic process—if the concurrent dysgenic effects can be fended off—are bound to require many, many generations. Meanwhile it may be expected that the world's population will have reached its crisis stage, as predicted, and some kinds of drastic measures for controlling the numbers of childbirths will have been taken throughout the world. The People's Republic of China, now with a population of one billion, is showing how those controls should be imposed through moral suasion and birth control measures such as contraception and abortion. However plausible the proposals for eugenics may seem, the potential effectiveness will surely be modified by the unknown and unpredictable condition of mankind one or two centuries from now.

Visions of a genetically improved society achieved in a shorter time than required by social planning are prompted by research in genetic surgery, therapy, or engineering. Such hopes are based upon the widely and often sensationally publicized accounts of techniques which may be employed to modify the genetic composition of the fertilized germ cells in a prospective mother. One purpose in using these highly sophisticated procedures would be to enable the fetus to develop into a child free of the disability or disease from which it would otherwise have suffered, by correcting defective genes at the earliest stage of development. A second purpose would be to predetermine the sex of the child by modifying the cell. And a third purpose, more spectacular and debatable than the others, would be to bring about the exact replication of, say, the father by inserting the nucleus of one of his somatic cells into the fertilized cytoplasm of the ovum in place of the original nucleus. This would cause the growing cell to be exactly of the phenotype of the father, and in due course of birth and growth the son would be a true replica of him. Indeed, theoretically, several such replicated offspring could be produced by this method. To be sure, it is a theoretical idea, however much success with frogs has been reported. While the prospect of cloning seems to have caught the fancy of the great public mind more than any other potential product of genetic manipulation, its very possibility is rejected by many competent scientists. "I fancy I hear in the distance," said Dr. Leon Eisenberg of Harvard Medical School, "the laughter of the gods at our hubris in speculating on the psychopathology of clonal man, a creature who is likely never to exist.[18] The more credulous scientists, who do not listen for the gods' derision, include Joshua Lederberg and James D. Watson. Everyone might justly hope that the applied science of genetics can eventually reduce the number of people who are victims of the unhappy conjunction of dangerous mutants and hereditary genes, and that right-thinking people will increasingly cooperate with counselors to avoid further mishaps. Still there is an almost universal dread of the possible misuse of genetic techniques in such way that human evolution would be made to veer away from the norm of truly human quality instead of moving closer to it. The ancient experiences of the ambiguity of human nature with its propensity toward both good and evil make genetic scheming seem rather problematical. Without significant moral improvement of the human race, in other words, the possible good of employing genetic knowledge only for physical health remains a limited value. This improvement, if it comes, will be signaled by a reversal of most people's lack of concern for the well-being of future generations. We despoil the earth, kill thousands of excellent young men as well as other civilians in warfare, and allow thousands or millions more to starve to death or die prematurely for causes which could be obviated. We provide our children with a heritage of ever more devastating weapons of destruction, and with social and political weapons which carry the seeds of still greater destructiveness. In view of this culpable disregard for the welfare of coming generations, is there any reason to have confidence that we will exercise a reasonable and charitable "genetic duty" toward the improvement of the whole race? No discussion of the social consequences of genetic science makes sense apart from the realistic struggle with these awesome questions.

Speaking in the broadest category of truth on this whole issue, the grandson of Charles Darwin, bearing the same name, observed, "Man can now aspire to the complete mastery of nature, but subject to the one condition that he can master himself." It will continue to be a major purpose of Christian faith and ethics to show men and women how the mastery of self is contingent upon service to all, both to those now living and those who are yet to experience their brief time upon

111

this planet. Else the tremendous benefits which are potential in such scientific advances as those of microbiology will be perverted and rendered impotent.

PRENATAL DIAGNOSIS

Even though it is most unlikely that a democratic society will adopt a comprehensive program of positive eugenics enforced by the state, a number of perplexing problems of orthogenesis, or right procreation, confront us. Some of these would not be problematical, were it not for the scientific and technological means which offer unprecedented options. Prior to modern—that is very recent—genetic and obstetric knowledge, some alternatives would not have been available at all.

To be sure, there has prevailed for generations the discreet, common sense advice given to brides and grooms who came from families in which noticeable diseases of body and mind were prevalent. Without the kinds of resources that are now available, however, congenital diseases most often went unchecked. Men and women ran unknown risks, even when they knew of the diseases in their own families. Children in those families may have died very young of biochemical deficiencies such as PKU (phenylketonuria), anemia, or galactosemia; of neural dysfunctions such as spina bifida (myelomeningocele); or of the nemesis of the Ashkenazy Jews from East Europe, Tay-Sachs disease. Others may have matured and lived with their families as blind, epileptic, "queer"; or as suffering semi-invalids with cystic fibrosis or muscular dystrophy. Still others with diabetes or hemophilia may have been known for the delicacy of their health and the limitations on their desires for normal activity.

In countries of high population and low economy, or where technologies for public health, medicine, and pediatric care are undeveloped, prospective parents still lack the genetic knowledge or assistance which might minimize or prevent further troubles. Childbirth is in every respect "natural," and often disappointing or distressing.

Genetic counseling in some countries is now on the increase as an option with valuable potential. Numerous men and women can testify to its benefits. In practice, however, it is not quite so effective as theory might promise. Several reasons account for the present deficiency. One is unavailability; another is expense. Moreover, relatively few men and women seem able to understand the simple Mendelian laws of genetics or the more complicated theories of inheritance. They may either feel intimidated by the counseling process, recklessly decide to ignore the counselor's advice, or suffer anxiety over the lack of a child. Finally, human fallibility accounts for errors in advice which may be given, or for personal bias which the counselor may inject, even unconsciously, into the advice. As Dr. Robert F. Murray, Jr., of Howard University observes, "Genetic counseling like medicine is part art and part science."[19] A purely objective, impersonal scientific diagnosis of the genotypes of a man and a woman is not to be expected. The science keeps growing and the art maturing. Dr. Hymie Gordon notes that just as surgery was once practiced by barbers, so genetic advice was "left to the local zoologist or anthropologist or to some other biologist."[20] However, the counselor today, if adequately educated and experienced, can succeed in meeting Dr. Gordon's three requirements: a precise diagnosis, a knowledge of family histories, and knowledge of up-to-date genetics.

Art and science also combine in the social programs of genetic screening in a given segment of population. Initiative is not left to individuals or couples; but some state laws require that certain people, especially infants and children, be examined for abnormalities which might prove to be dangerous. These apply especially to PKU and sickle-cell anemia. When this is compared to mandatory screening of whole populations for infectious diseases such as syphilis, malaria and small pox, it seems both logical and commendable to screen for congenital diseases. But, again, theory is better than reality.

The counseling given on the basis of data of family histories alone can deal in possibilities or probabilities. But for some genetic impairments the counselor can give exact predictions. These are the ones detected by testing the cells of a fetus *in utero* or by otherwise observing the condition of the developing unborn child. Techniques for such examination are becoming known to the public. Amniocentesis, though a technical term, has entered the vocabulary of journalists, who no longer see the need to define it. Readers know that it refers to the process of piercing the womb with a needle and extracting amniotic fluid for laboratory assay. This procedure may be preceded by using a device for scanning the fetus with sound waves and producing an ultrasonograph, which shows whether the unborn are twins, where amniotic fluid is concentrated, and whether there is critical neural tube impairment. Still more palpably, examinations of fetal tissue are made by using fetoscopy. With a needlelike viewing device, samples of blood and even of skin can be drawn from the fetus directly. Most recently, testing the pregnant woman's blood for alpha-fetoprotein is used to reveal the condition of spina bifida. (See p. 145.) Without detailing the many disorders detectable, it can be noted with amazement that more than three hundred genetic and chromosomal diseases can be diagnosed by these methods. And the researchers keep adding to that list.[21]

Intrauterine diagnoses can be done about the sixteenth week of gestation. The methods are considered reasonably safe, although not perfectly so. Experience already shows a risk that a fetus will be injured by the needle or fetoscope, and some subsequent spontaneous abortions are attributed to the procedures. However, as is often emphasized, the results of prenatal diagnosis are overwhelmingly positive and reassuring. In 95% of the cases, parents are relieved and happy to learn—for sure—that their developing child is a healthy one.

And what of the unhappy 5%? If prenatal diagnosis soon becomes a part of standard service in countries with well-developed health services, the gross number of that 5% minority will be large. And large indeed will be the emotional and moral problems they encounter. These are already identified and discussed in medical and ethical literature.

The commanding issue for many persons is abortion; for some it is no problem at all. In between those who say a categorical No or Yes to abortion are those who find either answer fraught with pain and anxiety. Hypothetically, even the one most concerned, the unborn child with indicated defect, might agonize over opting for death or life.

The particular issues are quite evident.

Will the genetic impairment prevent the child from ever having a meaningful life? (Whatever "meaningful" means!) Will it know only imbecility, severe physical disability, incontinence, constantly recurring pain, unrelieved medication or surgery, blindness, parental and sibling abuse? Will it be committed to a Bedlam-like institution when parents

114

cannot or will not provide home care? Will death come surely and early?

For parents and families, can the strains—emotional and financial—of caring for the child be borne? Will there be love for it? Is there already an impaired invalid in the family? What effect will the child's plight have upon the personal character development of others, and upon the careers of parents and siblings?

If abortion is chosen, will it be followed indefinitely by thoughts of guilt and remorse? Will it bear subsequently on the love-relation of wife and husband and other children?

Very often our minds are made up for us on complex questions by the repeated hearing and reading of certain phrases, in which the problematic word is conjoined with the acceptable one. This is the effect of the phrase, "amniocentesis with selective abortion," which is often used. It conveys two spurious ideas which gain by repetition. First, it automatically and inextricably links abortion with the diagnosis, leaving no room for decision against abortion. Second, the word "selective" implies an option which in reality is not expected to be offered, though it sounds like a choice.

The World Council of Churches' consultation on genetic issues, held in Zurich in 1973, noted that already then (and increasingly)

> in some medical centres amniocentesis has been conditional upon a woman's promising in advance to undergo an abortion should an affected fetus be diagnosed.[22]

But the participants, who were mainly geneticists and physicians, objected:

> The requirement of such a promise imposes a heavy burden upon parental decision-making and excludes from the benefits of amniocentesis those patients who are uncertain about or presently opposed to abortion.[23]

At the M.I.T. conference the judgment was added,

> It is contrary to the integrity and freedom of the couple or woman involved to require an abortion should amniocentesis reveal abnormalities.[24]

Those who take a strong "pro-choice" position on abortion might question the propriety of requiring a choice before the evidence can even be known.

The Zurich consultation proposed one criterion for the abortion decision which was rejected by the M.I.T. conference. It was suggested that "the increase in the load of detrimental genes in the population" resulting from "the reproduction of carriers of genetic diseases" would have a debilitating effect upon the entire gene pool of the human race.[25] Some do argue this point as a matter of one's moral responsibility to society. But is it a cogent argument? One geneticist, who favors abortions, nevertheless discredits this idea: James V. Neel of the University of Michigan sees no effect being made upon the whole pool, or sea, of genes.[26] M.I.T. biochemist Jonathan King and the French geneticist Jerôme Lejeune asserted the same opinion at the Conference. (It was Professor Lejeune who in 1959 first described the causes of Down's syndrome, widely and vulgarly called by the white racist name Mongolism.)

Abortion following diagnosis is no more "selective" than any other freely willed abortions. The fundamental, much disputed, question of the human nature of embryonic and fetal life, prevails in all discussions of the legitimacy of abortion. Yet the justifying causes are, for some minds, different here than in other instances. There is necessarily a difference of timing. Since amniocentesis cannot be performed usefully before the sixteenth week, the abortion may have to be done by Caesarian section or the repugnant injection of saline solution to induce labor. People who condone abortions in the early weeks often balk at those in later weeks.

In cases of abortion of both healthy and affected fetuses, according to American law since 1973, no reason other than the woman's wish and the physician's concurrence is required. There may be unexpressed reasons of great cogency, such as manifest medical necessity, early adolescence of a pregnant girl, or total inability to support the child. Or the choice may be made for the "convenience" of the woman, who has her personal reasons.

With genetic defects, however, the genuine concern may well be for the welfare of the child itself. In blunt truth, people can judge that prenatal denial of life is better than allowing a grossly impaired one. They can also express sincere concern about the high cost in both money and people, a cost which families and public institutions must meet for the lifetime care of mentally and physically incapacitated people.

Those who sense neither human care nor moral ambiguity in abortion are spared the agonizing experience of persons who are sensitive to them. Persons who deplore and resist abortion, but who are optimistic about genetic and medical science, can hope for the coming of more effectual therapeutic procedures which will enable infants to overcome some defects.

The main burden of responsible care, for the sake of human respect and love, must fall to men and women who insist that each unborn child, regardless of genetic health, be brought to birth into the human community.

The spirit of Prometheus, when chastened, will be expressed in the efforts to channel the energies of life and the powers of the mind toward the beneficent evolution of this unique species.

NOTES

1. Robert Heilbroner, *An Inquiry into the Human Prospect* (New York: Norton, 1974), p. 143.

2. Horace Freeland Judson, *The Eighth Day of Creation* (New York: Simon and Schuster, 1979), pp. 173–75.

3. Ibid., p. 110.

4. J. William Schopf, "The Evolution of the Earliest Cells," *Scientific American,* 239, no. 3 (September 1978): 114. The notable achievements of Dr. Arthur Kornberg and Dr. Har Gobind Khorana in synthesizing molecules of a virus and a yeast alanine are still not the same as "creating life." See D. S. Halacy, Jr., *Genetic Revolution* (New York: Harper and Row, 1974), p. 177.

5. François Jacob, *The Logic of Life,* trans. B. E. Spillman (New York: Random House, 1976), p. 16.

6. Robert L. Sinsheimer, "The Prospect of Designing Genetic Change," *Engineering and Science Magazine,* California Institute of Technology, April 1969, p. 8.

7. Hans Jonas, "Toward a Philosophy of Technology," *The Hastings Center Report,* 9, no. 1 (February 1979): 41. (Italics added)

8. Lewis Thomas, *The Medusa and the Snail* (New York: Viking Press, 1979), p. 73.

9. Ibid., p. 157.

10. Paul D. Saltman, *The Implications of the Chemical-Biological Revolution* (Grand Forks: University of North Dakota, 1967), p. 7.

11. Clifford Grobstein, *A Double Image of the Double Helix* (San Francisco: W. H. Freeman, 1979). See the analysis of the problem of fixing recombinant DNA research guidelines in June Goodfield, *Playing God* (New York: Harcourt Brace Jovanovich, 1977), chap. 7.

12. *Faith and Science in an Unjust World,* vol. 2 (Philadelphia: Fortress Press, 1980), pp. 53–54.

13. P. B. Medawar, "Genetic Options: An Examination of Current Fallacies," *Life or Death: Ethics and Options,* ed. Daniel H. Labby (Seattle: University of Washington, 1968), p. 105. Other critical appraisals of the theory and practice of positive eugenics are discussed in Mark H. Haller, *Eugenics* (New Brunswick: Rutgers University, 1963); Donald K. Pickens, *Eugenics and the Progressives* (Nashville: Vanderbilt University, 1968); Kenneth M. Ludmerer, *Genetics and American Society* (Baltimore: Johns Hopkins University, 1972).

14. Hermann J. Muller, *Studies in Genetics* (Bloomington: Indiana University, 1962), p. 517. Muller's ideas are expounded in "What Genetic Course Will Man Steer?" *Man's Future Birthright,* ed. E. A. Carlson (Albany: State University of New York, 1973), pp. 117–52.

15. Theodosius Dobzhansky, "Human Values in an Evolving World," *Human Values and Advancing Technology,* ed. Cameron P. Hall (New York: Friendship Press, 1967), p. 61. See also his essay, "Living with Biological Evolution," *Man and the Biological Revolution,* ed. R. H. Haynes (Toronto: York University, 1976), p. 34. Despite this criticism of Muller, Dobzhansky did affirm principles of eugenics by signing the Edinburgh "Geneticists' Manifesto" in 1939. See Muller, *Studies in Genetics,* p. 548.

16. Paul Ramsey, "Moral and Religious Implications of Genetic Control," *Genetics and the Future of Man,* ed. J. D. Roslansky (Amsterdam: North Holland Publishing Co., 1966), p. 147. Republished in his *Fabricated Man* (New Haven: Yale University Press, 1970), chap. 1.

17. Theodosius Dobzhansky, "Human Values in an Evolving World," p. 64.

18. Leon Eisenberg, "The Psychopathology of Clonal Man," *Genetics and the Law,* ed. George J. Annas and Aubrey Milunsky (New York: Plenum Press, 1976), p. 387. See also *Journal of Medicine and Philosophy* 1, no. 4 (1976): 318–31.

19. Robert F. Murray, "Ethical Problems in Genetic Counseling," *Genetics and the Quality of Life,* ed. Paul Abrecht and Charles Birch (Elmsford: Pergamon Press, 1975), p. 173; see also his "Screening: A Practitioner's View," *Ethical Issues in Human Genetics,* ed. Daniel Callahan (New York: Plenum Press, 1973), pp. 121–30.

20. Hymie Gordon, "Genetic Counseling," *Journal of the American Medical Association,* 217 (August 30, 1971): 1223.

21. Oliver W. Jones, "Prenatal Diagnosis of Birth Defects," *Perinatal Care,* 1, no. 4 (November–December 1977): 10–17; Mitchell S. Golbus et al., "Prenatal Genetic Diagnosis in 3000 Amniocenteses," *The New England Journal of Medicine,* 300 (January 25, 1979): 157–68; Laurence E. Karp, *Genetic Engineering: Threat or Promise?* (Chicago: Nelson-Hall, 1976), chap. 5.

22. Abrecht and Birch, *Genetics and the Quality of Life,* p. 204.

23. Ibid.

24. *Faith and Science,* vol. 2, p. 51.

25. Abrecht and Birch, *Genetics and the Quality of Life,* p. 207.

26. Cited in John Fletcher, "The Brink: The Parent-Child Bond in Genetic Revolution," *Theological Studies,* 33 (September 1972): 482.

5 ...and Keeps Rebounding/ Dilemmas of Conception and Birth

AIDS TO PROCREATION

Among the many ironies and paradoxes which constitute human existence is this one: while some people will do anything to avoid having children as the consequence of sexual pleasure, others use any means to have them, even without sexual union. One woman's pregnancy seems a disaster, another's her most desired fulfillment. Procreative technology now offers some fulfillment of both wishes: sex without babies, or babies without sex. (This use of the word *sex* is the popular and crude designation of copulation or intercourse, being of the same level of usage as "having sex" instead of sharing its complementary powers.) There are widely accessible means of separating sexual intercourse and procreation, isolating either one or the other, and thus interrupting the natural continuum between them.

The mere mention of this paradox opens the door to an unruly crowd of clamorous and angry moral debaters. "Sexual union is for procreation, not recreation," argues one group. "Birth prevention is a great invention," say others. Should the reception of contraception be warmly appreciative for the joy of sex? Or is contraception a deception for human beings who with pro-life conviction should be more prolific?

The Conference at M.I.T. opened the door slightly to two big issues of this category: fertilization without intercourse, either within a woman's uterus or in a glass dish; and the care of newborn babies with genetic diseases and deformities. It did not allow to come through that door the large, bristling abortion argument with all the legal, psychological, social, and theological questions sticking to it. So it is not to be fully discussed here.

121

INSEMINATION BY SYRINGE

One aid to pregnancy is AID (artificial insemination by donor). This form of artificial insemination is less personal than AIH. When H stands for husband the delivery of sperm by artificial means poses fewer moral problems—and for many people, none—than does impregnation by the gamete of a donor. To be realistic and literal, though, this anonymous donation of semen is no gift at all; it is sold to the woman, the physician serving as a middleman in this commercial transaction. To describe this so is not necessarily to judge it, any more than one necessarily condemns the selling of one's blood for transfusion.

The bicentennial of artificial insemination in 1976 was somewhat overshadowed by that of the United States of America. Even so, the textbooks commemorate Lazzaro Spallanzani who in 1776 first succeeded in helping a female dog on the way to motherhood by this simple method. Within two decades, a certain John Hunter gathered human sperm and attempted to do the same for a woman.

In America today more than 60% of all cattle are bred by what may be styled AIB, the bull being of prized pedigree. If it is good for developing strains of meaty, disease-resistant animals, why not also for human beings? This is the way the positive eugenicist asks the rhetorical question. But thus far, the use of AID for humans has not been so motivated; and for AIH it could not be so in any case, since the husband's chromosomes are the same no matter how they reach and fertilize the wife's ovum.

If not "to improve the stock" of one's family or humanity at large, why do women opt for AI? At least five reasons are generally recognized.

Primarily, of course, a woman wants a child: by the husband's semen if normal intercourse does not succeed; by that of another man if the husband's infertility suggests such.

The new techniques of freezing offer a second option for AIH. If a man decides to have a vasectomy in order permanently to limit procreation, he may first deposit his semen in a cryogenic bank. Then in the event of such an emergency as the death of his only child, the couple will still have the possibility of reproducing.

In instances where the blood types of the couple are incompatible—

she being Rh-negative, he positive—another man's sperm may be used. The same reason applies to the avoidance of genetic diseases known to be carried by the husband. In all cases of AID where the intention is to avoid such risks, it is now assumed that the husband agrees to the process and is willing to accept the resulting child as his own. Some laws rule out complications on this point by requiring the husband to sign a consent form if the child is to have the same filial rights as a natural or adopted one.

In the fast-moving progress of procreation technology, researchers have recently found a way to avoid the natural randomness of producing boys and girls. Gender is determined by the chromosomes in the male's sperm, not by those in the female's ovum. But individual spermatozoa differ: some contain the X chromosome (female) and some the Y (male). If there were a way to separate these two types, it would be possible by AI to predetermine the gender of offspring. Now there *is* a way, though its availability is minimal and its results inadequately evaluated.[1] In more advanced stage of development today is the technique of identifying gender in a sixteen-week-old fetus by using amniocentesis. Although the justification for a deliberate abortion of the unwanted sex is morally debatable, it is a practice which has already made a start.

Upheavals in the social mores regarding sex relations, sexual morality, and the emancipation of women from traditional roles are manifestly having much bearing upon the uses of AI. Conversely, AI is contributing directly to these moral changes, simply by being a viable option. Questions of morality, propriety, and legality are rapidly arising. Should a physician provide AID for an unmarried woman? For one of a pair of lesbian women? Women can argue on firm legal grounds that they, as individual citizens, are as much entitled to bear children as are married women. This would hardly be a new phenomenon. In a much-noted survey by M. Curie-Cohen and associates, which at this writing is the most recent one, 10% of the nearly five hundred physicians questioned said they are providing AID to unmarried women.[2] In one such case, where the father's identity was well-known to the woman, a judge (in New Jersey, 1977) awarded to the man the right to visit the resulting two-year-old boy, though contrary to the mother's wishes.[3]

These five reasons for artificial insemination are of uneven gravity. Disregarding the perverse and lurid publicity given by mass journalism to bizarre cases, what estimates can we make of them?

Moral judgments made on the basis of Christian beliefs about sexuality and parenthood are not uniform. Roman Catholic teaching is the clearest, most consistent, and most reserved. It prohibits AID in every case and formally disapproves AIH, though with some flexibility to meet urgent needs.[4] Those who are not Catholics may admire the resolute effort to hold the moral line against the excesses of promiscuity, exploitation, perversion and degradation of human sexuality, and to uphold the integrity of marriage and parenthood. However, moral casuistry often is carried to the extreme limits of reasonable acceptance. AIH is formally repudiated by the church because it violates the integrity of the procreative relationship of marriage and inevitably requires the husband to masturbate; AID is equated with the sin of adultery. As Lutheran theologian Helmut Thielicke shows, both of these Catholic objections disregard the element of intention, so essential to a credible Christian ethics. The husband intends to help his wife, whom he loves, have a child. The woman does not intend anything like an adulterous relation to an anonymous seller of semen. Thielicke's own estimate of AID, by the way, is also negative. He sees it as a pernicious undermining of authentic parenthood and personal relations under God. But the alternative which he suggests to childless couples is a rather pathetic commendation of adoption, which in the present time of birth control and extensive abortion has become difficult for people who want children of their own kind.[5] (Although many orphans of the world need parents to adopt them.)

The bishops of the Anglican Communion in 1958 took a two-dimensional view:

> The Christian rightly accepts the help of responsible physicians in making conception possible where it may be prevented by some physical or emotional abnormality. Artificial insemination by anyone other than the husband raises problems of such gravity that the Committee [of the Lambeth Conference] cannot see any possibility of its acceptance by Christian people.[6]

These opinions of two church bodies are not arbitrary. They rest upon the biblical doctrine of human creation and dignity, in which the sexual capacity for procreation is treated with respect and monogamous marriage is normative. While modern knowledge of the biology of human reproduction far exceeds that of any preceding generation, it does not necessarily mean that such knowledge abrogates the traditional insights, but complements or modifies them. The question for the churches is not: How can liberal scientific morality replace prudish prescientific rules? but: What is really best for humanity's maintenance of the divine image and all that implies for life?

The Report of the World Council of Churches at M.I.T. was fully permissive about AIH. It expressed a grave concern about the artificial separation of procreation from both marriage and sexual union, but it recognized also how some Christians can "accept AID as a legitimate and compassionate solution to human need" when a husband is sincerely willing to be fatherly toward the child so conceived. As to AID for unmarried women, however, the Conference said of Christian teaching: "Children are a blessing for the married couple, and awareness of the importance of a father for a child suggests that such insemination is unethical."[7] Too often the good of the child is ignored in these discussions.

One need not go to the churches to find critical appraisals of AI, however. Physicians and lawyers have their own questions to raise, as do psychologists and legislators.

Various jurisdictions are trying to clarify the status of children born after AID. Are they de facto adopted by the couples? Are they illegitimate, and thus subject to the hindrances and public embarrassments of bastardy, which our society has failed to alleviate thus far? If a woman secretly becomes pregnant by AID with the help of a physician, what moral and even financial responsibility should the physician bear in the event the husband refuses to accept the child? And what if the child should suffer a serious genetic defect putatively from the anonymous father?

In the present time of marital confusion, sexual license, and the disposition of unhappy patients to sue their physicians for malpractice, these questions are not theoretical or trivial ones.[8] Even more demanding of legal clarification are the frozen sperm banks, which at present operate without regulations under an assumed policy of free enterprise.[9]

A writer on medical law, George J. Annas of Boston University, designated a number of ills needing urgent correction, after he had read the Curie-Cohen report. Most of the problems are due to two deficiencies: the lack of carefulness by the physicians and the lack of medical and legal regulations.

There is little genetic screening of donors for AID. As is well-known, these are usually medical students, who, to put it crudely, are willing to masturbate for money. The current rate is twenty-five to thirty dollars. Medical students are conveniently available, they do not have to be told what it is all about, and often they are impecunious. One might muse on the idea, however, that AID is not a medical matter but a seminal one, so sperm could appropriately be secured from seminary students as well. As Annas judges, "current practices are based primarily on protecting the best interests of the sperm donor rather than those of the recipient or resulting child."[10] Moreover, most general practitioners and many gynecologists are not qualified to do the genetic tests. "On the whole," reported Curie-Cohen, "most of our respondents showed poor knowledge of genetics."[11]

A deceptive way of using AID to give the suggestion that the possibly infertile husband may indeed be the father is to mix his sperm with that of others.

Contrariwise, a willing donor may be, and is, used so often that he becomes the biological father of very many children, possible a hundred, it is reported. In smaller communities rather than huge cities, this has already caused suspicion that some young men and women have unwittingly committed incest in their legal marriage. As a person with human sensitivities, does this fecund donor ever wonder who his sons and daughters are? As sensitive human beings with the presumed right of knowing their parentage, what is the traumatic effect upon children, psychologically and spiritually, when they learn that their father was Anonymous Donor?

The survey shows that relatively few physicians keep adequate records of these procedures; many have only a brief and passing professional relationship to the women concerned. Therefore, scarcely any follow-up studies are made to determine the physiological and psychological sequelae of AID.

In light of the critical views of expert judges of AID as currently practiced, the statement of the World Council of Churches Conference

126

is not unduly apprehensive and cautionary: "It may well be feared that the use of such techniques would lead further to the depersonalizing and dehumanizing of life."[12]

HUMAN LIFE IN A GLASS

The millions of people who follow scientific news may not know anything of the fast-disappearing language of Latin. But they know that in vitro fertilization of a human ovum means that an egg is fertilized by a sperm cell in a glass dish, or test tube, rather than in the woman's womb. And it has survived and developed when placed back in the woman. Baby Louise Joy Brown's birth on July 5, 1978 brought joy to the world of obstetrical science and to thousands of women who for various reasons are unable to conceive a child by normal methods. The day should be remembered as one of those decisive dates in human history. What its implications for the future may be can only be guessed at, not clearly foreseen. Whether this "blessed event" will prove to be a mixture of blessing and something worse is now being debated. In any case, the present reality of this healthy, growing girl whose origin was effected outside her mother's body by scientifically facilitated in-ovulation—and of two other babies so conceived in India and Scotland —guarantees the coming of more babies and more problems.

An old Latin motto says *in vino veritas,* that is, in wine (there is) truth. It suggests a phrasing for the basic question about this procedure: *in vitro humanitas?* that is, in glass (is there) humanity? For this is the much disputed moral issue which divides people over the legitimacy of this wonder of reproductive technology.

On the first birthday of Baby Louise the participants in the "Faith, Science and the Future" Conference were trying to decide whether there is a "Christian position" on in vitro fertilization (IVF for short) with embryo transfer to the woman. This was not the first such discussion under auspices of the World Council of Churches, nor the last to come. Highly qualified persons meeting at Zurich in 1973 could not even discover a common conscience and judgment on "the deliberate culture of human embryos in order to use and then destroy them for experimental purposes."[13] Dr. Robert G. Edwards of Cambridge University took part in the Zurich study. It was he who collaborated with Dr. Patrick Steptoe in Oldham, England to assist Mrs. Brown in this first-of-its-kind pregnancy and birth. Edwards later commended the Zurich consultation on its permissive, though not unanimous, position.[14] At M.I.T. the delegates were somewhat more guarded about endorsing the ingenious and problem-laden procedure. They admitted the obvious truth that IVF could lead to some benefits for childless married couples and for reproductive research. The reservations they expressed were mainly of a practical nature rather than of a philosophical or theological kind. It would be better, they said, to expend scientific skill and resources for determining why the fallopian tubes, or oviducts, of some women become blocked, and then direct more research toward correcting the malfunctions. Further, said the report, resources would be better deployed for meeting the health needs of large numbers of poorly served people than helping the relatively small number of women who want to bear babies. As for the inevitable problems of humanity in the glass, the report simply poses questions. It takes no position. What are the limits of experimentation with zygotes or embryos? If a child born of this method is deformed, who bears responsibility? What about transferring one woman's fertilized ovum to another woman's womb for gestation?

Churches and their moralists apparently have not had time to formulate policy statements covering these and similar issues. Indeed, they are still trying to catch up with other rapidly changing conditions in society and in medical practice which challenge traditional, simplistic moral judgments about sexuality and procreation, genetics, health services, and aging and death. The rush of events cannot wait for recognized definers and defenders of Christian morality to make up their divided minds. As for the population in general, the *Washington Post* editorialized: ". . . the time for society to begin seriously thinking about these issues has long since come."[15] In America, the government's Department of Health, Education and Welfare (HEW), which like a cell in mitosis divided into two departments in 1979, has carried on a deep probing study of IVF. An Ethics Advisory Board of thirteen experts of appropriate disciplines and professions, well served by a staff, took testimony from dozens of witnesses.[16] Meanwhile, public hearings were held in the Commonwealth of Virginia on whether to allow the Norfolk General Hospital to prepare a special clinic and offer

IVF services to women with fallopian fallibility. (Permission was granted in January 1980.)

In all these arenas the same kinds of questions, charges, and rebuttals have been arising. It is thus possible to take a synoptic view of the range of them without discussing each in a separate context. In matters where people's conceptions are polarized, it is helpful to arrange the Yes and No considerations in parallel columns, thus comparing them and weighing their relative cogencies.

YES to IVF	NO to IVF
1. The "right of married couples to have a child has been established unequivocally" in United Nations' declarations, wrote Dr. Edwards as the justification for his work.[17] He interprets this by mentioning that "attempts to establish eugenic controls have been unpopular."	Article XVI(1) of the United Nations Universal Declaration on Human Rights specifies the right "to found a family." This really means that couples have the right *not to be prevented* from having the family they want, not to be helped to procreate. Likewise, the United States Bill of Rights guarantees "the right to bear arms" but not to be armed by someone.
2. Married couples who want to be parents are at least deserving of such assistance as IVF provides.	The world is dangerously overpopulated already, as every demographic survey shows. Some justify abortions for this reason. Why go to extreme, expensive efforts to add to the population problem?
3. It is widely agreed that IVF should be, and will be, made available only to married couples. This is specified in the HEW proposed guidelines as "lawfully married" and in the Norfolk protocol as "stable married couples."	Marriage has become increasingly unstable in Western Europe, Britain, and North America. Considering the social trends, there is no reason to doubt that IVF will be extended to unmarried women, to the employing of sperm from anonymous donors (AID), and to the implanting of blastocysts (embryos) in surrogate ("hostess") mothers. It is most doubtful, too, that law

129

4. There is no need to have moral concern for the fertilized egg in the Petri dish at zygote stage, nor as a morula or blastocyst. Whether people perceive it to be mere cellular tissue or potentially a human being but not yet protectible, 50–60% of all pre-embryos fail to become implanted in the uterus where they can survive and grow.

courts will uphold exclusion of unmarried women from IVF.

The zygote is the beginning of a new and unique human being, even at its minute size; a Christian or humanitarian belief in the sacredness of human life mandates both respect and protection. The same strong inhibitions against abortion apply to IVF. Furthermore, it is unavoidable to assume that impregnated women will be examined after sixteen weeks with a view to aborting defective fetuses. The fact that many embryos and fetuses are aborted spontaneously does not justify abortion at any stage. People die naturally too!

5. Religious and moral sensitivities are changing as people become better accustomed to the revolution in procreative science and practice. Once the practice of IVF has become known and accepted by the public, people will lose their objections to it, as they have with AID and abortion, infanticide, and euthanasia.

Belief in the sacredness and inviolability of human life at all stages of development is so integrally bound to the Christian understanding of God's creation of humanity that it must be held without condition or change.

6. IVF for humans has been adequately tested by experimentation with animals and by long experience with the artificial breeding of domestic animals. Risks to women and to children so conceived are no greater than in normal childbearing. These babies which have been born are healthy. Nevertheless, the risks of abnormality will be mitigated by amniocentesis or fetoscopy and

Sufficient experimentation with nonhuman primates has not been done with time to observe results.[18] Dr. Steptoe himself admitted that of 32 implantings only 4 pregnancies resulted, and only 2 came to term. (Mrs. Brown's first pregnancy was unsuccessful.) It is too early, after only a few births, to express confidence in the efficiency of the procedure and the normalcy of the children.

the option of aborting defective fetuses.

It remains too risky.[19] As for the reliance on abortion as a check to deformity, that is highly problematical, to say the least.

7. Clinical use of IVF for helping childless couples will yield important information, otherwise unavailable, on genes, sex determination, effects of drugs, and fetal development. Moreover, experimentation without intention of transferring the embryo to a woman's womb must be done to promote techniques of much value for childbearing women in the future.

It is obvious that the line between clinical and experimental use is most difficult to discern.[20] In the name of research, it will be an irresistible temptation for some investigators to maintain embryos in vitro as long as possible and undertake experiments which are morally questionable or reproachable.

8. The cost of IVF service is relatively low when compared to the inestimable value of having one's own child. (The Norfolk clinic estimates $4,000.)

Even at $4,000 the cost makes IVF a privilege of the few and beyond the means of childless poor couples. More serious, considering the strong desire for children and willingness to pay any price for IVF, practitioners will make of it a profitable enterprise.

9. There is sufficient justifiable human benefit by IVF to warrant the investment of the resources of hospitals, physicians and other health professionals.

Because of limited availability, IVF (if considered morally acceptable) would violate any principle of equitable distribution of scientific and medical resources.

10. IVF is good medical practice, treating the disability of fallopian tube obstruction or disease. It is therapy. For psychic health some women and men truly need to have children.

IVF is not good medical practice but biological technology; it is contrary to "accepted medical ethics."[21] It is a service to people's desires (like cosmetic surgery) rather than a treatment of their illness.

11. Christians should see that it is in accord with God's will for

Many Christians of all church traditions regard IVF as contrary

131

humans to use their reason and skill to complement the work of creation and the operations of nature; they do this by myriad kinds of life-enhancing techniques.

to the natural law instituted by God which connects sexual union with procreation. Just as contraception separates sexual union from procreation, so IVF (and AID) separate procreation from sexual union.

12. The division of opinion among Christian theologians and church leaders renders invalid any judgment which is simply labeled "Christian." IVF's acceptability is vindicated by a variety of beneficial considerations.

Despite their lack of unanimity, Christians should employ their reasoned judgment and take moral positions according to their consciences and (in many cases) in congruence with the teachings of their churches.

13. Legislators, policymakers and lawyers can cope with any legal issues as they arise, such as tort cases involving birth defects attributed to IVF.

Legal problems will certainly arise, and they will prove to be extremely complex and difficult to resolve. The more procreative technology develops new and strange techniques, the less likely are laws, lawyers, and judges able to help people who suffer various kinds of damage.

Thirteen main points of disagreement provide the docket for an extended debate; this is precisely what has been initiated by the achievement of Drs. Edwards and Steptoe. Did the doctors know on how many sensitive toes they were stepping? If not, they soon learned of the extent and intensity of opposition, as well as the surging wave of support. In this context it may be useful to comment on only certain of the thirteen disagreements.

2. The anguished expressions of married couples reveal a depth of feeling which others would not know without hearing such men and women personally. Despite the irony of rocketing rates of abortion and declarations of certain feminists on the joys of being unencumbered by children, a large proportion of women sense what the Old Testament called their reproach for being childless. When Elizabeth, the middle-aged mother of John the Baptist, rejoiced in her fifth month of

pregnancy, she exclaimed, "Thus the Lord has taken away my reproach among men" (Luke 1:25). She must have remembered the 113th Psalm: "He gives the barren woman a home, making her the joyous mother of children. Praise the Lord!" There is pathos in the sight of Hindu and Buddhist women offering sacrifices to gods for the sake of their fertility. So it is asked about married women seeking IVF, will their cherishing the desire for offspring not guarantee they will be good, caring mothers? And yet there is a psychic risk for those who have their fertilized oocytes returned to their bodies. The risk is even deeper disappointment and depression if they are among the (at present) large majority of women who still fail to become pregnant or carry a pregnancy to term.

4. The human identity, moral inviolability, and legal protectibility of the fertilized ovum, before and after its successful implantation in the lining of the uterine wall, remains the nub of the argument over the deliberate termination of any pregnancy. In the United States and other countries having no legal prohibition against abortions, or at least early abortions, the legal question has been resolved for the present. Only a reversal by the highest courts of their decisions, or an amendment to their basic law or constitution, can alter the legal nonprotectibility of the embryo or fetus.

After hearing stentorian speeches at pro and anti demonstrations, enduring endless and inconclusive low-key conversations, reading editorials and letters to the editor and tracts and learned articles and books and even smoke-writing in the sky—one despairs of any real communication. Yet minds do change through it all, and converts are made to either side. Rhetoric, slogans, and symbols play their part. Ironically, a sweet baby face symbolizes both the pro-IVF and the antiabortion forces. Perhaps in a more sinister way, the symbol for proabortion (or "pro-choice") should be a metal coat hanger; and for the anti-IVF, the drain pipe of a sink. Crude? Yes. But this is how many people feel and understand the loggerheaded debate. Minds can become blocked more readily than oviducts.

Perhaps the HEW Ethics Advisory Board came as near to a median view as is currently possible:

> After much analysis and discussion regarding both scientific data and moral status of the embryo, the Board is in agreement that the human

133

embryo is entitled to profound respect; but this respect does not necessarily encompass the full legal and moral rights attributed to persons.[22]

It was by reference to this policy statement that the Board responded to subsequent inquiries about the legitimacy of doing laboratory research with fertilized ova in vivo. And that is simple Latin for a human egg, fertilized by normal sexual union, growing in the womb of the mother-to-be!

5. As to rapidly changing attitudes, these are plainly evident to anyone who has matured since 1950 or so. Beliefs and convictions change; ideas and prejudices change; social pressures and federal laws change; technologies for the beginnings and endings of life change. Yesterday's shocking outrages have become agreeable subjects for television shows and advocacy by religious bodies. Is the evidence now in hand to demonstrate that most Europeans and Americans can assimilate almost any contradiction of past morality? It is on the basis of that cynical (or some would say, hopeful) assurance that defenders of IVF say, "Just wait." In respect to this and related issues affecting human life, its dignity and support, many writers use the metaphor of the wedge. Drive it a little into the oak log of custom or morality, hammer it a bit further, and the log starts to crack and split. As long as the force is applied, hardly anything can stop the wedge.

Some experts who are not accused of rhetorical overkill use this image very soberly. This is how IVF has come to its present stage, implies Marc Lappé:

> The original purposes of perfecting in vitro techniques—to study the physiology and maturation of critical organ systems and to understand the processes where development goes wrong (teratogenesis), have been largely abandoned by these latter-day efforts to put technological innovation directly into clinical practice. And it is here that a major ethical omission has occurred.[23]

7. If the human embryo in its earliest stages, less than a week after fertilization of the ovum or at that much disputed "moment of conception," is worthy of "profound respect," what does this imply for in vitro experimentation? Some investigators hardly give the question of a zygote's intrinsic value a moment's thought—until they seek funding

from the government. Then they realize how profoundly many people do respect that cluster of growing cells.

Minds become trapped in their own subtleties. First they think IVF with embryo transfer must be opposed because it has not been sufficiently tested with human procreation. Then they consider experimentation needed for testing to be morally wrong because it puts the embryo at risk. Since there is no morally acceptable way of testing, therefore, it is better to place a ban on IVF altogether.

The negative view of experimentation is hardened by suspicion that some investigators, given the means, are ready to go far beyond the limits of human propriety, mixing the germ plasm of human beings with that of animals. Experiments have already been funded by HEW which involve the joining of human sperm with the eggs of rats, mice, and hamsters. One of these concentrates on the binding of the sperm of a boar to the egg of its mate and is described as follows:

> When human ejaculated sperm, or rat or guinea pig cauda epidydimal sperm, were added at high concentration (ten times higher than the boar sperm controls) and stimulated to high motility by caffeine, they failed to bind to porcine oocytes.[24]

No comment was written to express disappointment that the human sperm failed to perform as well as the sperm of golden hamsters and bulls.

Persons who exercise regulatory and financial control over the uses of human germ plasm need at times to walk an ethical razor's edge, and especially so when fertilized ova are being used.

8. Two kinds of questions have been posed concerning the financial aspects of IVF with embryo transfer. First, should there be public funding for it? Evidently the answer is now affirmative in Australia, Austria, Denmark, India, and the United Kingdom; but negative in the United States. Pressures are strong to convince people and their elected legislators that this is as legitimate a medical procedure as any other for which payments are made. Second, the suggested price of $4,000 occasions a situation of rather tragic irony for poor women of the land. One poor woman complains, "I want to have, and must have, an abortion, but I can't afford it." Another poor woman and her husband say, "We want to have a child by in vitro

fertilization, but we can't afford it." Is there a connection between these two instances? Would public funding for the former necessarily include the latter, too?

12. Even though religious ethical thinkers are being placed under duress to resolve the problems involved and to formulate guidelines to judgment, it seems unlikely that moral policies on IVF will avoid the fate of the ones now focused on abortion. Even the consistency of the Roman Catholic teaching is uncertain here. When asked about the "test tube baby," the Catholic Bishop of Cork, Cornelius Lucy, remarked, "Offhand, I don't see anything wrong with childless couples using the test tube method if there is no other possible way for them to have babies." But the Catholic Bishop of Augsburg, Joseph Stimpfle, declared dramatically, "Technical manipulation with human eggs and sperm is worse than the atom bomb!"[25] How much less are the prospects of accord among Protestants needs no explanation. The issues are so complex that no prominent theologians or churchly teaching office can successfully lay down the law.

The divided mind of Christians especially, but also of Jews and humanists, was illustrated by the testimonies of religiously motivated men and women presented to the Ethics Advisory Board and at the hearing at Norfolk, Virginia. Merely to assert a categorical Yes or No to IVF was less effective at last than to specify reasons and conditions for approval or disapproval. The case of the Norfolk clinic is the most instructive one so far, though others will undoubtedly arise. Here there was no claim on public funding, only permission to renovate the clinic. The physicians were admonished by some speakers that a high ethical respect for human life and dignity would require the following conditions:

1. Only one ovum will be extracted (not "harvested"!) from a woman's ovary at a time. Dr. Steptoe used hormones to cause super-ovulation and thus secured many ova at once with which to work. Perhaps they were "cheaper by the dozen"; but there was consequent cheapening of human respect as well, if eleven of twelve resulting zygotes were not intended to be implanted.

2. The service of IVF with embryo transfer will be provided only to reasonably stable married couples, and with their due informed consent.

3. No zygote's life will be unduly prolonged outside the uterus. Three days are normal for reintroducing the embryo, and fourteen days are suggested by the Ethics Advisory Board as the maximum.

4. Neither a donated ovum from a second woman, nor implantation of the zygote in a second woman will be practiced.

5. Research will be limited to the observations made during the IVF process itself, with the sole purpose of assisting pregnancy.

6. No prior commitments by the parents for abortion will be included or required in their giving consent.

The reasons for these conditions are neither self-evident nor unambiguous. However, taken together the conditions constitute a practical restraint upon any use of in vitro which is psychologically or morally questionable.

HUMAN REJECTS ON THE REPRODUCTION LINE?

Despite technological improvements on nature, the making of babies is still done in the conventional way by most women. Even in the highly mechanized societies there is a growing interest in natural childbirth and a disencumbrance of technological assistance; this is happening just at the time time when artificial aids to childbearing are increasingly effective and available. Somehow the ancient notion remains deeply embedded in the human subconsciousness that nature knows best how to help mothers.

There is a formidable disability in nature's way, however, and its consequences bring much anguish and tragedy. It is the frequency of aberrations in the health of babies during their prenatal growth. Some of these are caused by the ignorance or carelessness of the pregnant women or those attending them. Having abandoned the gross superstitions about the damaging effect of environment upon the developing child, women who once held them are learning of the effects which are by no means a matter of superstition or magic, or even of some divine intervention. They are the defects caused by chemical actions on genetic instructions. Neither the penetrating glance of an enemy's "evil eye" nor the relative locations of the planets in their solar orbits can determine what kind of child will eventually emerge

137

from the dark womb to light and visibility. Neither are the chances of a child's becoming a concert violinist or flutist enhanced significantly by the expectant mother's frequent listening to recordings of Mozart and Telemann. If she imbibes too many alcoholic drinks, however, or smokes too many cigarettes, there is now being reported an increasing body of evidence that her child will be adversely affected before birth. The effects of drug use to the point of addiction can be much worse, or the inadvertent and sensational malformations which were caused twenty years ago by such untested sedative drugs as thalidomide. Now the prevalent fear is of X-rays and atomic radiation. In these and other ways, *human* nature, with its curse of either unwilled or willful ignorance, intrudes upon what is regarded as an otherwise benign course of natural development toward the birth of normally healthy girls and boys.

Nature has her own ways of disrupting the hopes for having babies which are free of physical or mental impairments. She does not need the bumblings of prematernal behavior nor external physical attacks upon the suspended fetus to cause the immeasurable distress and tragedy of birth defects. The chemical codings of countless genes determine what kind of human being each embryo will become. Any slight distortion, imbalance or mutation of the genes, which first may have occurred inexplicably several generations ago, can cause very grave damage to the growing child. Only within the three or four recent decades have biologists and geneticists come to understand the reasons for numerous defects. They may have been identified a century ago and their effects described; now they are being scientifically understood in such concrete detail that many can be remedied. Yet the tragedies of parental disappointment and infant distress continue. Persons of naively credulous religious belief, especially anguished mothers with shattered hopes, have traditionally thought that defective infants were caused by the intervention of supernatural powers. Either a judgmental god was using the occasion to mete out vindictive punishment for sins; or else a demonic or satanic power was invading the womb for its own devilish reasons. Such belief is crass superstition. It has nothing to do with the faith taught by reasonable Christianity and Judaism. Certainly, the frequent incidence of birth disorders gives rise to the deepest and most perplexing questions for faith and theology about the relation of evil to the power of a loving Creator. Job and Jesus are of far more help here than Prometheus, but even they finally leave the questions unresolved. A mother's lament, "Why has God done this to me?" however sincere and poignant, implies a concept of divine cruelty or retribution which does not belong to this religious faith.

Back to nature—as the name for the processes of creation—we note that she is famous for wastefulness. In the reckless prodigality of germ plasm, thousands of fish eggs are spawned—of which many are eaten or otherwise destroyed, as are countless minnows hatched from them—in order to assure that a dozen will reach mature fishhood with the capability for further reproduction. With human eggs, nature is parsimonious. A woman can ovulate at most about 400 times, and only a dozen or so of her eggs will be fertilized. With spermatozoa it is a different story, hundreds of millions in each man are lost. Despite nature's thrifty care for fertilized ova, there is in the totality of the human race a vast quantity of offspring which come to nothing. One-half or more of zygotes at the 64-cell morula stage fail to find secure uterine implantation. It is theorized that a very high proportion of these failures serve to eliminate at the outset the embryos which are already genetically defective and thus doomed to anomalous growth. This is a form of natural selection for the good of the species. Moreover, the tiny embryo's chances of healthy development and eventual birth are formidably impeded by a host of genetic barriers as well as by abortions, both spontaneous and deliberate. In truth, it is a wonder that as many babies survive as do reach childhood.

Geneticists have served the cause of their swiftly growing branch of science by identifying and describing at least three thousand possible disorders.[26] These are syndromes of many kinds, usually with polysyllabic technical names, affecting at least 3% of the newborn babies in America and comparable numbers in other lands. Not all the diseases are understood; or, we say, are not *as yet* understood, since the state of the art is not static. Nor are all genetic malformations of the same gravity. Some bring a continuing lifelong inconvenience to persons because of minor physical handicaps; others cause horrible deformities and are incurably lethal. Even within one disease there may be wide variations of morbidity. For example, babies afflicted with the common Down's syndrome may vary considerably in bodily health and coordination; and their eventual IQ may range from an idiotic 25 to a rather self-sufficient 80.[27] Some cases of genetic disorder can be successfully treated, ameliorated, or passably corrected by medication, special diet, surgery, prosthesis, or just loving care. Others are of such pathological gravity as to defy any therapeutic treatment at all.

The three thousand or more types which have already been identified fall into four main classes:

The metabolic disorders, which disrupt processes of food assimilation and cell growth. Cystic fibrosis, galactosemia, Tay-Sachs disease, and Huntington's chorea are of this type.

The sex-chromosome and X-linked diseases cause mental or physical deformities, or both. The Lesch-Nyhan syndrome, Duchenne muscular dystrophy, and the cutaneous disease, ichthyosis, are among the eighty-six known kinds.

Chromosomal irregularities, or translocations of chromosomes, cause such conditions as the prevalent Down's syndrome.

Neural tube defects are congenital malformations of the spinal column, seen especially in spina bifida (myelomeningocele), which is treatable, and anencephaly (headlessness), which is literally hopeless.[28]

The classification, pathology, and modes of therapy for these affected newborn infants is a new science which has generated a high amount of technical literature, as well as a body of mature popular books which describe the disorders and discuss the difficult problems and dilemmas they pose.[29] Women and men anticipating parenthood must become informed on these matters today, whatever their views about natural childbirth may be.

Those who are personally and socially concerned about the many complex issues raised by birth disorders should be on guard, however, against facile generalizations about them. Recognizing hundreds of specific varieties as well as the variations and gradations of intensity within particular types, we cannot assume the applicability or wisdom of uncritical statements of judgment about them all. Of course, the categorical assertion that *every* genetically or accidentally injured fetus should be aborted or, if brought to term, be allowed to die is a generalization which at least exhibits the virtues of simplicity, consistency, technical nationality, and concern for population eugenics and public economy. It also reveals, in the minds of those who make it, a total disregard for the mystery of life and the intrinsic value of individual human beings.

There is an ironic way in which the fact of visibility exerts opposite effects upon people's emotional and mental attitudes toward the fate of both the unborn and the imperfectly born. To see someone is to have a personal experience of him or her. To read or hear about someone, or a class or persons, usually means to have only a mental impression. Therefore, on the one hand, people who readily approve abortions are said to be condemning human beings because they are invisible. Many would change their attitude, it is argued, if they could see the recognizable human fetus of ten weeks or later in the womb of its mother. But it is not likely for a person to feel genuine sympathy for a fetus when it is just an abstract idea, or just an intrusion or invader threatening a woman's well-being. On the other hand, it is claimed, people who passionately advocate the use of extraordinary means of preserving the lives of severely affected newborn infants might change their minds if they could actually see these pitiable creatures in their hopeless conditions. Both accusations contain only partial truth, but probably enough to account for the views held by great numbers of men and women.

During the World Council's conference at M.I.T., a woman physician from Nairobi asked a perplexing and disturbing question. In traditional African culture, she said, it was the custom to kill defective newborns because it was believed that they were little monsters, possessed by evil spirits. When Africans became Christians, they were told by missionaries that such children should be cared for and saved if possible because as humans they are the gift of God. "Now, what are we to say," she queried, "when we see Christians in Europe and America permitting genetically affected infants to be aborted after diagnosis, or left to die after birth?" Her question was not posed in a sarcastic or defiant mood, but in one of sincere concern to know the answer. Who could reply? Of course, one could point to the relatively high rate of infant mortality in African countries today as a justification for concentrating the limited resources of pediatric care upon healthy infants, while neglecting the others which are most likely to die anyhow. But that rationalization of the "let die" policy is a theoretical one which fails to account for two sets of facts. First, there are many varieties of diseases and defects, as mentioned above, which defy generalization. Second, the rapid advances in the knowledge of genetic epidemiology and therapy can be, and are being, made known in the developing countries.

As to the first consideration of varieties, it might be added that under the broad category of birth defects there are important differences in circumstance, or context, of the affected baby and not only diversities of kind and intensity of the disorder. The Kenyan doctor's question had point with respect to some, but not all, of these three conditions:

Abortions for reason of moderate and possible corrigible defects discerned in the fetus.

Babies born by parental choice even after the prenatal diagnoses have revealed their troubles.

Those born with defects which were neither predicted nor expected by parents and obstetricians. Of course, some are literally born dying with fatal afflictions: some will die soon unless appropriate medical or surgical care is given quickly; some will die inevitably before the lapse of a known number of months or years. But some have the strength to survive indefinitely under varying conditions of handicap.

There are two critical questions in each case. Are the medical/surgical/technical means available to this child? Do the parents and physicians want to use those means to give the infant the maximum chance of continued life and development?

In countries where medical technology is less developed and not easily available to women, the deformed or diseased baby is most likely to become just another statistical unit in the high rate of infant mortality. If it fortunately avoids that pathetic exit from the human community, protective care by the extended family is more to be expected than where there is more technological, but not necessarily human, development. For better or worse, and probably for better, there is seldom an option for institutionalization. Yet, early child care is gaining in places where it was introduced only recently. In Nigeria, as an example, sickle-cell anemia, which affects adversely the flow of blood through capillaries, has always been prominently manifest among black people. In the 1950s, according to Dr. A. Eyimofe Boyo, it was impossible to find children more than two years old with the sickle-shaped cell. Today, because of early child care with the use of antimalarial drugs and folic acid treatment, many such children grow to maturity and normal activity.[30]

What of infants being born in societies which provide modern medical and surgical services, including intensive care units for newborns? How do parents and health professionals decree the fate of these abnormal and sometimes grotesque babies? (If they survive and are educable, they may be known euphemistically in the presently accepted usage as "exceptional children.") Again, no easy generalizations apply, but difficult choices must be made. In some states in America, if the parents and physicians do not decide to apply all means of therapy, the courts may rule that they must. In others, the attending physicians and hospital staff may, with parental consent, disregard with impunity even some laws of homicide, or in this case infanticide, and by "benign neglect" allow salvageable infants to die.

Most persons involved in the birth of an "exceptional" infant are aware that they are also involved in moral and legal dilemmas of broad social importance. For some, the experience may seem merely perplexing. For others, it is a genuine, insoluble, and deeply disturbing dilemma.

To be involved professionally in the specialty of assisting the birth of impaired infants necessarily involves one in moral and legal problems of baffling complexity and broad scope. Parents, family members, pastors, and counselors and the attending medical personnel become in each case members of a temporary community of anxiety. The psychological and economic problems of the family only add to the burden of having to resolve the perplexing decisions of life and death. While these are perplexing for some, they are true dilemmas for others, impossible to resolve satisfactorily.

The more the combined techniques of neonatology are improved and practiced, the more difficult becomes the task of caring for the increasing numbers of children surviving with severe handicaps.

143

It is possible, of course, to avoid the parents' perplexities and the doctors' dilemmas in what seems to be a simple manner. This just requires undeviating, sincere adherence to the belief that neither the fetus as diagnosed nor the baby as observed has any inviolable claim on a continuing life. Many people no doubt agree with Robert G. Edwards's blunt statement: "I find great difficulty in accepting the notion . . . that sacredness of life is sufficient reason to avoid aborting all foetuses with severe genetic defects."[31] And the Nobel Laureate, James D. Watson, has been quoted many times since 1973—with approval, too—as saying that infanticide should be considered licit within the first three days after birth. A similar question is posed by British writer Robert Reid, "whether parents have a right to bring defective children into the world when methods of early diagnosis of the condition are available."[32] Acknowledging the United Nations' defined "right" of every married couple to have a child, Reid believes that the combined "right" of the child "not to be unfairly burdened" and the parents' "right" to avoid such burden outweigh together the parents' "nonright" to burden society with an expensive defective child. So which "right" is right?

Such permissiveness toward death and seeming indifference to the "right" of a fetus or infant to live if at all possible may be due to certain factors.

One is the eugenic ideology of physical perfection, which was discussed in the preceding chapter. It is an appealing aristocratic view of human potential, which was propounded in Athens of ancient time, long before the existence of genes was suspected. If Prometheus had not spurned Pandora, but married her and decided to raise a nuclear family, he would—if living today—know exactly how to employ procreative technologies to guarantee unblemished progeny.

In the porcelain factory of Nymphenburg Palace near Munich the finest quality plates, cups, and tureens are made by expert craftsmen, just as they have been made since the eighteenth century. Each detail is done to perfection. But when the inspector's practiced eye detects even one slight fault, which others would hardly ever see, he smashes the beautifully painted and glazed creation. No seconds are sold here. Only perfection is acceptable.

Where does the eugenicist draw that critical line? If the impossibility of true perfection is acknowledged, as it must be, what degree toward it is tolerable? The practitioner's art of discerning in each case the proper medical indications is not yet guided by a calibrated scale of human worth or of "indicators of humanhood."[33] However pressing the need for criteria just now, no schema so far proposed merits a very wide acceptance. Physicians dealing with neonatal diseases doubtless have their criteria of survival value in mind. These are minimal standards of tolerable imperfections, however, rather than maximal ones for adjudging perfection. So it has to be. The cliché, none of us is perfect, is not just a lame excuse for one's poor work, but a truly profound statement about human beings as such. It happens to coincide with the long-honored biblical view of humanity as well.

Another influential factor shaping one's judgment about neonatal defects is the humanitarian concern to avoid causing people more distress and suffering than they can, or should, bear. No one doubts or dodges the reality of pain, despair, and even prolonged agony which such diseases cause. How heavy is that "unfair burden" to infant, family, society?

The example of dealing with cases of spina bifida generally illustrates the cleavage of ideas and attitudes among professionals. In the center of the debate within the circle of obstetrics/gynecology/neonatology has been the Hungarian-born Dr. John Lorber at Sheffield Children's Hospital in England. His specialty is this neural tube disorder, also called myelomeningocele. It occurs with relative frequency in Britain and Ireland as a most dreaded disease. The flesh on the back of the child developing in the womb does not close over the spinal column, leaving either a large open lesion or forming a huge bulbous cyst. Soon after birth this condition forces spinal fluid to the head, effecting the enlarged condition of hydrocephaly with imminent threat of brain damage. Such an infant appears to be a hopeless "monster." Nevertheless, during the 1950s the Sheffield team of Drs. Robert B. Zachary, W. J. W. Sherrard, and Lorber demonstrated neurosurgical virtuosity in devising effective remedies. They closed the wound on the newborn's back or removed the cyst, then inserted a tubal shunt from the brain cavity to heart or stomach to remove the dangerous fluid. This method of veritable brain drain

145

along with dorsal surgery was adopted at many other hospitals. Hundreds of babies were thus saved from a certain early death. Lorber's follow-up surveys showed that by 1970 more than 40% of his young patients were alive, ranging from eight to twelve years in age. Though partially paralyzed and mostly incontinent (some with mental retardation), some were attaining what has come to be called, without definition, "meaningful life." Even so, Lorber pondered the fact that the more babies which were being repaired for survival, the heavier became the burden to families—domestic, financial, emotional—and also to the budget of the National Health Service. This so troubled his mind that he resolved henceforth to help only those babies which his experienced eye could judge to have optimum chance of living. From the rest he would deliberately withhold treatment, not only allowing but willing them to die in days or months. He explained his decision carefully to the perplexed parents, finding most of them in agreement. Meanwhile, the amniocentetic test for diagnosing spina bifida and its worst manifestation, anencephaly, was devised.

Dr. Lorber's senior colleague, Dr. Zachary, disagreed sharply with this policy. His lectures and papers demonstrated how many infants so afflicted could be assisted eventually to lead lives of personal, intellectual, and social value, albeit as partial invalids. Some Americans also challenged Lorber's hard line in reporting their own successes.[34] The tragic cases continue, despite early abortions. However, as Zachary's epigram states the issue and the motivation for treatment: "The fundamental purpose is not to add years to their lives but to add life to their years."[35] This is not a sentimental slogan, but a stern rejection of any disregard for the value and defensibility of human lives which, despite high cost and suffering, need not be invariably lost or destroyed. In effect, it is a protest against passive euthanasia for infants. As he conjoins the problem of letting-die with that of abortion following adverse diagnosis, he comments:

> It has often been said by those who oppose abortion that the disregard for the life of a child within the uterus would spill over into the postnatal life. This suggestion has been "pooh-poohed," yet spina bifida is a clear example of this. The equanimity with which the life of a 17-week gestation spina bifida infant is terminated after the finding of a high-level of (alpha) fetoprotein in the amniotic fluid has,

I think, spilled over to a similar disregard for the life of the child with spina bifida after birth.[36]

Yes, it is more than a problem. It is a dilemma for which no moral precept or legal code can provide a happy solution. This impasse should neither astonish nor frustrate us. Mortal life in human society is replete with unavoidable dilemmas. This just happens to be one which troubles the sensitive person's conscience more than others. Of course, each infant's case of live or die can be relativized almost to triviality by seeing it in the context of the world's macropathology. The much advertised "birthquake" and "time bomb" of population growth is as grave as they say it is. So are the present and threatening rate of starvation and the ultimate menace of nuclear war. The four apocalyptic horses still ride across the earth, not as eschatological fancies but as all too real phenomena of pestilence, war, famine, and death. But these overwhelming considerations do not prescribe to physician, nurse, and parents what to do in the maternity ward with this particular child.

Let the law decide, say some. Laws there must be to govern such questions. However, law professor R. A. Burt believes rightly that nuances and flexibilities of both law and morality must of necessity be acknowledged. In accepting "the relatively haphazard application of the criminal laws regarding treatment of newborns . . . it is enough to see that certainty of application would require us either to press enforcement to end all purposeful withholding of treatment for newborns or to establish that someone in this society has clear authority to end some infants' lives."[37] Considering all relevant factors, we are left in the marginal cases with what may only be "the best choice among bad choices."

NOTES

1. "Sex Selection before Child's Conception," *Journal of the American Medical Association,* 241 (March 23, 1979): 1220.

2. M. Curie-Cohen et al., "Current Practice of Artificial Insemination by Donor in the United States," *New England Journal of Medicine,* 300 (March 15, 1979): 585–90.

3. "New Jersey Judge Gives Donor of Sperm the Right of Visits to Woman's Son," *New York Times,* July 22, 1977.

4. Bernard Häring, *Ethics of Manipulation* (New York: Seabury Press, 1975), p. 195. For a contrary and permissive estimate of AID by Catholic theologians see A. Kosnik, *Human Sexuality* (New York: Paulist Press, 1977), p. 138.

5. Helmut Thielicke, *The Ethics of Sex,* trans. John Doberstein (New York: Harper and Row, 1964), pp. 255–59.

6. *The Lambeth Conference, 1958* (London: SPCK, 1958), p. 148.

7. *Faith and Science in an Unjust World,* vol. 2 (Philadelphia: Fortress Press, 1980), p. 52.

8. See David G. Lygre, *Life Manipulation* (New York: Walker and Co., 1979), Chapter 2 and extensive bibliography.

9. At the annual meeting of the American Association for the Advancement of Science, Houston, Texas, January 6, 1979, proponents and entrepreneurs of human semen cryobanking not only admitted the absence of standards but pled for regulations to protect what they regard as the inherent values of enterprise.

10. George J. Annas, "Artificial Insemination: Beyond the Best Interests of the Donor," *The Hastings Center Report,* 9, no. 4 (August 1979): 14. In respect to carelessness about ascertaining genetic history, a doctor who surveyed the practice quotes an "obstetrician of international reputation" as saying, "It's alright, because I know the sperm is gotten from donors who are graduate students" (Richard M. Restak, *Pre-Meditated Man* [New York: Viking Press, 1975], p. 71).

11. M. Curie-Cohen, "Current Practice of Artificial Insemination."

12. *Faith and Science in an Unjust World,* vol. 2 (Philadelphia: Fortress Press, 1980), p. 51.

13. Paul Abrecht and Charles Birch, ed., *Genetics and the Quality of Life* (Elmsford: Pergamon Press, 1975), p. 211.

14. Robert G. Edwards, "Fertilization of Human Eggs in Vitro: Morals, Ethics and the Law," *The Quarterly Review of Biology,* 49 (March 1974): 380.

15. January 19, 1980.

16. Ethics Advisory Board, Department of Health, Education and Welfare, *HEW Support of Research Involving Human In Vitro Fertilization and Embryo Transfer,* Washington, D.C., May 4, 1979.

17. Robert G. Edwards, "Fertilization of the Human Egg," p. 381.

18. HEW Ethics Advisory Board Report, pp. 39–42, 104.

19. Clifford Grobstein, "External Human Fertilization," *Scientific American,* 240 (June 1979): 61. He concludes: "The safety issue for the fetus therefore, is not fully resolved, and can only be further assessed through additional testing and experience."

20. LeRoy Walters, "Human In Vitro Fertilization: A Review of the Ethical Literature," *The Hastings Center Report,* 9, no. 4 (August 1979):

23. This study was executed for the Ethics Advisory Board of the Department of Health, Education and Welfare, 1978.

21. Paul Ramsey, "Shall We Reproduce?" *The Journal of the American Medical Association,* 220 (June 5, 1972): 1350. "Either the accepted principles of medical ethics must give way, or fabricated babies should not be ventured."

22. HEW Ethics Advisory Board Report, p. 101.

23. Marc Lappé, "Ethics at the Center of Life: Protecting Vulnerable Subjects," *The Hastings Center Report,* 8, no. 5 (October 1978): 12.

24. Rudolph N. Peterson et al., "Sperm-Egg Enteraction: Evidence for Boar Sperm Plasma Membrane Receptors for Porcine Zona Pellucida," *Science,* 207 (January 1980): 74.

25. Quoted by Richard A. McCormick, S.J., "Notes on Moral Theology: 1978," *Theological Studies,* 39, no. 1 (March 1979): 100.

26. Aubrey Milunsky, ed. *Genetic Disorders and the Fetus* (New York and London: Plenum Press, 1979), p. 289.

27. Marc Lappé, *Genetic Politics* (New York: Simon & Schuster, 1979), p. 119.

28. Following the classification in Milunsky, *Genetic Disorders*; the work gives a detailed and comprehensive bibliography.

29. Robert Reid, *My Children, My Children* (New York: Harcourt Brace Jovanovich, 1977); Virginia Apgar and Joan Beck, *Is My Baby All Right?* (New York: Trident Press, 1972), p. 176. The latter is strictly descriptive, avoiding the mention of abortion and death.

30. A. Eyimofe Boyo, "Sickle Cell Disease—Life or Death?" Abrecht and Birch, *Genetics and the Quality of Life,* p. 151.

31. Robert G. Edwards, "Judging the Social Values of Scientific Advances," Abrecht and Birch, *Genetics and the Quality of Life,* p. 49.

32. Robert Reid, *My Children, My Children,* pp. 165–67; also, anonymous, "Let Blighted Babies Die or Not?" *Medical World News,* November 17, 1972, p. 27.

33. Widely discussed are the provocative "indicators of humanhood" suggested by Joseph Fletcher, *Humanhood, Essays in Biomedical Ethics* (Buffalo: Prometheus Books, 1979), pp. 12–19.

34. Mary D. Ames and Luis Schut, "Results of Treatment of 171 Consecutive Myelomeningoceles, 1963 to 1968," *Pediatrics,* 50 (1972): 466; Rosalyn B. Darling, "Parents, Physicians and Spina Bifida," *The Hastings Center Report,* 7, no. 4 (August 1977); 10–14; Anonymous, "Children with Congenital Spine or Limb Defects Can Be Rehabilitated," *Journal of the American Medical Association,* 238 (December 19, 1977): 2677–79. Dr. John Lorber's explanation of his policy may be read in his article "Selective Treatment of Myelomeningocele: To Treat or Not to Treat," *Journal of Pediatrics,* 53 (March 1974): 307–88. A critical al-

ternative to his policy is by John Freeman, *Practical Management of Meningomyelocele* (Baltimore: University Park Press, 1974). An ethical analysis of their dispute is by Stanley Hauerwas, "Selecting Children to Live or Die," *Death, Dying and Euthanasia,* ed. Dennis J. Horan and David Mall (Washington, D.C.: University Publications of America, Inc., 1977), pp. 228–49.

35. Cited by Paul Ramsey, *Ethics at the Edge of Life* (New Haven: Yale University Press, 1978), p. 184. Ramsey's critical discussion of the spina bifida complex of ethical problems merits most careful reading, whatever the view or persuasion of the reader (pp. 181–98).

36. Robert B. Zachary, "Life with Spina Bifida," *British Medical Journal,* December 3, 1977, pp. 1460–62.

37. R. A. Burt, "Authorizing Death for Anomalous Newborns," Aubrey Milunsky and G. J. Annas, eds., *Genetics and the Law* (New York and London: Plenum Press, 1976), p. 447.

6 | Have *We* the Energy?

A REVIEW OF FOUR VIEWPOINTS

Certain particular convictions have come to predominate in the preceding discussions. They were not present as self-evident propositional truths before considerations were given to the selected problems of science, faith, and ethics. Whenever attention is directed to specific problems of the uses of technology, natural environment, genetics and the new techniques affecting conception and childbirth, a variety of options have to be looked at. At first glance, it may seem that one viewpoint is as valid as another, or else that these problems are so complex and baffling that the wisest course is to withhold decisions and continue to look for more wisdom. The reader may think this, and maintain the thought even after the second and third glances as well. But to be a mature person requires one eventually to favor a certain judgment or position which warrants actions.

The difficulty is compounded when one tries to think as a Christian. This does not mean abandoning personal intellectual responsibility, asking only, "What does the church teach about this?" or "What is the prevailing view of leading theologians?" These are obviously important and useful considerations, but not decisive ones necessarily. A man's or woman's integrity of mind and conscience can be sustained only in response to the question, "What can *I* understand about this issue in the light of relevant scientific data and the conceptions of faith and theology which I have come to hold?"

During this process of study and writing, some ideas which at first seemed right and adequate were modified; and some which had not been possessed with certainty or perceived in clarity were confirmed

151

and elucidated. To the writer, in retrospect, four of these stand out most prominently: a critical optimism concerning the potential uses of technology according to human and humanizing values of freedom, responsibility, and fulfillment; a respect for the interpenetration and interaction between Christian faith and the array of modern sciences, at times in conflict, at times in constructive concord; advocacy of the careful exercise by all human beings of dominion over the rest of living and inert nature, or creation, as the given privilege held in trust from the Creator; adherence to the nearly, but not quite, absolute value of each human life as it is threatened, controlled, modified, or enhanced by emerging techniques.

For reason of space limitation, insufficient attention has been paid to the social, economic, and political dimensions of these scientific and technological issues. Such must be pursued in some other context, for obviously the uses and abuses of all forms of technology are influenced by varying kinds of policies and programs of action. These are devised and advanced by governments, by strong commercial interests (either private or state controlled) and by such powerful public institutions as professional associations, labor unions, research institutes, universities, and religious bodies. Motivations of competition for power and profit, or of promoting group interests and widest public good compel people to take strong stands on these and similar matters. This means that in all but the most regimented societies the people need to use their freedom, of whatever degree, to struggle for the expression and advancement of their concerns for social justice, tolerable economic equity, and ecological stability. Finally, the nation states of the world are linked to this chain of involvement, contending as they must for their own integrity and development within the parameters of global order and cherished peace.

Science and technology are in numerous ways related to all such dynamic forces of religious conviction, ideologies, popular and national interests, and the interaction of nations. In its studies of church and society the World Council of Churches has been endeavoring to take sober account of all these factors. It has thus been successful in the doubly difficult achievement of avoiding simplistic dogmatic pronouncements (such as people often, and deplorably, seem to expect of church groups) and still providing well-informed and reasoned guidelines to help all persons who are disposed to follow them in making up their minds.

The man who has directed this work for more than thirty years, Paul Abrecht, has been accorded highest compliments for having attracted into consultations and conferences women and men of competence and authority in the natural sciences, social sciences, and related disciplines, along with leading theological thinkers of the churches.

These people have adopted as the key words of aspiration and striving the interrelated objectives of justice, participation, and sustainability. The first two pertain to all people everywhere; the third to the earth and its biosphere as they now depend upon human care. Justice implies equity of the essential needs and primary opportunities of living for all human beings. Participation means the liberation of people from the powers suppressing the open expression of their minds in shaping policies which affect their own lives, as well as the initiative to use this freedom. Sustainability is the attribute of the planet itself, with all its marvelous, incalculable, and yet vulnerable resources for the indefinite sustaining of our human race, our animal companions, and the earth and water from which all things grow. These are ideal goals, to be sure, but not utopian fancies. They will never be achieved to perfection; but failure to attain them in rather high degree will spell ever increasing troubles in the future.

After many centuries of technical progress and self-assertion against the deities, Prometheus has run into severe trouble. Even *his* conscience is troubled by the power he has grasped. No longer is he stealing flint and tinder from the Olympians and enlarging thereby the powers of the mortals against the gods. Not with fire in his hands, but with the knowledge in his head of electrons, protons, neutrons, and high energy particles, he is nervously facing his own and humanity's perilous prospect.

Matter and energy are the two basics, and life is inseparable from them. From the light of the sun and its heat, from photosynthesis, gravitational pull, oxidation, growth of cells, on down to the electrical charges of the atoms, we are wholly dependent on energy. However, we are not simply dependent on these forces, we are manipulators of them as well. So technology brings us to the control of both human generation and nuclear-powered generators, to problems of genetic

153

breeding and of the breeding of plutonium. In this technological movement we are encountering still more dilemmas. The principle of a dilemma is simply stated: you can't have it both ways—not if the two ways are the opposite horns of the dilemma. We want uninhibited technological development as the population of the earth rapidly expands, and at the same time a steady increase of risk-free energy and power for the propulsion of that development. If we cannot have both, then what?

NOT, "HAVE WE THE *ENERGY?*" BUT, "HAVE *WE* THE ENERGY?"

As members of the one humanity, we need moral energy to match our intellectual energy if we are to harness the requisite physical energy for the just and participatory living which is sought for all. No doubt there are many people who do not as yet recognize this complex of energies. They may, in their unquestioning technolatry, believe that the heightened problems of insufficient, excessively expensive, and dangerous fuels can soon be solved by the physicists, engineers, and technocrats. This was the view of quite sophisticated people thirty years ago, when the roseate vista of "the peaceful uses of atomic energy" promised the fulfillment of all industrial and domestic needs. Those diminishing few who still cling to it should know that this is an utterly discredited illusion. The illusion has done more than evaporate into nothingness; it has transformed itself into a grave threat. David Lilienthal, who once chaired the Atomic Energy Commission, is quoted as having remarked, "Once a bright hope, shared by all mankind including myself, the rash proliferation of atomic-powered plants has become one of the ugliest clouds overhanging America."

It is not insignificant that church councils have emulated scientific societies and government agencies in giving high priority to the world's energy needs. Since the entire population is affected by ever increasing demands for fuel, the ambiguous good of the nuclear generation of such fuel both beckons and alienates. Not only the people living in countries having access to advanced mechanical and electronic technologies, but the great majority who live in simpler societies know that the difficulties of generating and distributing adequate supplies of energy are both disturbing and challenging. What is more, where atomic energy is concerned, the dangers are possibly of ultimate gravity.

If it were only a technological problem, there would be small reason for the troubling of consciences. It would still be a very difficult task, as shown by the disagreements of petroleum geologists, atomic scientists, engineers, and politicians about what can, might, or should be done to secure more energy. How long can the reserves of nonrenewable fossil fuels last? The question was already being asked in the 1940s but without much sense of anxiety. Americans generally were comforted by the confident belief that they would never live to see the time when supplies of crude oil and natural gas would give out or, next to that, become prohibitively expensive. They put their trust, not in the God who is honored on their coins, but in such friendly divinities as Standard Oil, Shell, Texaco, and Aramco. These were the gods from whom oil blessings flow. The deep wells of America's Southwest and the globe's Middle East would continue to provide gasoline at the pump for twenty cents a gallon. Few doubted that those faraway Arabs, backward but romantic, wearing quaint burnooses and riding camels across the hot sands, would continue to be the economic vassals of the Big Oil corporations.

Should the need arise, however, when crude oil might become uncomfortably expensive for generating electricity, it was calmly assumed that the new era of nuclear power would begin with safety and efficiency. School children were taught that there was enough energy locked in a lump of coal to drive an ocean liner for months—or, more accurately they found, in a hunk of uranium. True enough, nuclear-powered ships and submarines soon became a reality. So did the first generating plants.

It was assumed that the dreadful aspects of atomic energy could and would be nullified. As custodian of the Hiroshima-type bombs (equal in explosive force to a mere thousand tons or so of TNT), America would make sure that no irresponsible or hostile countries would ever be allowed to have them. That time of confidence in benign stewardship of the ultimate weapon lasted only a few years. The radioactive fallout from mushrooming clouds over Siberia, China, Rajasthan, and Tahiti began drifting with the trade winds of the earth. Nuclear reactors soon appeared in the United Kingdom and certain

European countries, which had the capability to make hydrogen and cobalt bombs but preferred to use their resources to meet domestic energy needs.

The third unexamined assumption thirty years ago was that the breaking up of colonial empires in Africa, Latin America, and Asia would simply involve the orderly transfer of governing authority to the independent but still docile leaders of the emerging nations. The British Commonwealth, Portugal, France, and the Netherlands would still exercise a pacifying and civilizing control over decolonialized peoples, while the economic colonialism of the United States would remain essentially beneficial for the new nations and profitable for American business.

The quarter century of history is not to be understood quite so simply as the foregoing sketch makes it appear. Even so, in retrospect we can see and lament the false assumptions, the naive optimism, and the surprising turn of events in those years. If the atomic age was born in 1945, it came of age in 1973, when suddenly the price of crude oil from Saudi Arabia, Kuwait, and kindred producers was quadrupled. The "energy problem" became for everyone the "energy crisis." Many Americans who had believed that "it can't happen here" found that it had. The nations belonging to the Organization of Petroleum Exporting Countries had come to the not so strange conclusion that the great deposits of oil beneath their soil and sand belonged to them, and not to foreign corporations.

Normally, many of us do not think about the vast breadth and depth of energy consumption in a nation or in the world at large. We pay our bills for fuel and electricity and say to the service station attendant, "Fill 'er up," with little more than a sense of irritation at the rising prices. Of course, our awareness is much keener than that if we are among the economically depressed people of society, especially the ill and aged, for whom the deficiency of heat in a cold climate can mean severe discomfort, even death. It is when our eyes can behold at one moment of time a vast and thickly populated area that we can sense, in other than an abstract way, what the dimension of energy needs are. On an exceptionally clear night when visibility is unlimited we may be flying in a jet plane, six miles above the earth's surface, from Tokyo to Hong Kong, Zurich to Amsterdam, Paris to London, or Boston to

Washington. Looking down, we see how humanity has spread like an illuminated carpet over the land. Lights by the millions! And behind the lights are office buildings, factories, blocks of flats and houses in which there are endless systems of electrical wiring, pipes with hot water, furnaces, and generators. Racing in every direction, are the lightbeams of thousands of automobiles, thirstily consuming fuel and lubricants which have come, mainly, by supertankers from ports of the Persian Gulf. Having such a graphic impression, we can better understand why the term *oil* has come to spell turmoil in Japan, Europe, and the United States. And we might be more sympathetic toward those whose attitudes since 1973 have varied—almost as in approaching one's death—among the emotions of initial panic, bitter anger, anxiety, self-pity, occasional resignation, and hope that some action can forestall the impending disaster.

One utterly reasonable and indispensable reaction which most people have thus far avoided, however, is self-restraint and effectual conservation. Six years after 1973, Americans were still importing one-half the petroleum they consume, and using up each year one-third of all the commercially available energy in the whole world. Very testily, the economist E. F. Schumacher, said, "It is obvious that the world cannot afford the USA," and added, "Nor can it afford Western Europe and Japan."[1] Ironically, during this same period the smaller, poorer, hungrier nations were being advised by economic experts that they should strive to become self-sufficient for their food and basic necessities.

The global vehicle is literally running out of gas. While there remain more than seven hundred billion barrels of oil as yet untapped as well as countless cubic meters of natural gas, the unrenewable fossil fuels may be expected to be depleted within just one generation if current rates of consumption continue and other major energy resources are not employed. Reserves of coal are still unthinkably vast; and yet they too are exhaustible if large industrial nations should convert their furnaces and generators to coal. In simpler economies where wood has traditionally been the primary fuel there is being enacted a "tragedy of wood." The imminent threats of deforestation have ecological and human consequences more dire and irreversible than the loss of shade trees on a hot day. All these examples of imminent de-

157

pletion have been fully investigated, charted, extrapolated, and quantified by scientists in every country. Their surveys add up to one unassailable conclusion: that a growing world population must turn to other sources of energy than oil and gas. That has meant, and still means atomic energy.

NUCLEAR, BUT UNCLEAR

If the pleasant dream of cheap, safe, clean, and inexhaustible energy derived from nuclear fission has proved to be more like a fitful nightmare, it is still part of the inescapable crash program to provide adequate alternatives to gas and oil. In the countries of Western Europe and America, where nuclear generators have already been functioning, the principle of participatory democracy has been demonstrated in wide-ranging debates about the nuclear future. Bumper stickers declare "No Nukes!" and hundreds of protesters lay down their bodies at the gates of nuclear plants under construction. Pronuclear advocates stick slogans on *their* cars—"Let 'em freeze to death in the dark!"—and send smartly tailored young executive types into airports to tell the passengers of the benefits of nuclear energy. Both sides do more effective work than those efforts, however, as they lobby in the offices of legislators for particular national policies. The British Council of Churches, the National Council of Churches in the U.S.A., other Christian groups in Europe, as well as environmental defenders of all kinds, have taken stands of either limited or absolute opposition to atomic energy.

Between Yes and No there is a Maybe; and the Maybe has nuances as well.[2] Those in the middle of the argument, which is so complex and important, need to examine very carefully the claims made by either extreme. After six years of intensive study and consultation, this is where the leaders of the Church and Society sub-unit of the World Council of Churches found themselves in 1979. Theirs was not a fence-straddling position due to craven indecision; it was a reasoned acceptance that a positive but qualified adoption of nuclear energy would be in the best interests of the just, participatory, and sustainable society they sought. It was rather a jolting change of emphasis, there-

fore, when the three hundred fifty delegates to the Council's conference at M.I.T. voted in favor of a five-year moratorium on the construction of nuclear reactors. This resolution was communicated by the
church officials to appropriate offices of government as an expression
of reasoned opinion. In the United States, however, it was not a radical
proposition, because the country began in 1979 a de facto moratorium
in the interest of further study on safety.

The arguments on this urgent issue are not just visceral or emotional,
even though they cause people to become excited and belligerent. However unsuccessful each side may be in persuading the other, their particular points of contestation need to be considered seriously for their
intrinsic validity and merit.

A Brief for the Pro-nuclear Position

1. Nuclear power is safe. The chances of catastrophic breakdown
are computed to be a million to one; and lesser kinds of malfunction or
damage can be contained securely. With seventy plants already functioning in the United States and about one hundred fifty in Europe,
Britain, and elsewhere, there has been no human fatality. No one was
killed in the breakdown at Flixborough in England, Creys-Malville in
France, or Brown's Ferry and Three Mile Island in the United States.

2. Nuclear power does not pollute the air to any extent comparable
to what oil- or coal-burning generators effect. The "thermal pollution"
of nearby rivers, due to cooling process, is being corrected.

3. Radioactive waste presents a difficult but not insuperable problem for safe disposal.

4. The use of plutonium 239 in the liquid metal fast breeder reactor (LMFBR) will prove to be a virtual "perpetual motion" of energy source, since it will extend the earth's supply of uranium energy-
use by a thousand times. Furthermore, plutonium waste is reusable.

5. Nuclear energy is, and probably will remain, the cheapest for all
concerned.

6. Experts agree that no alternate to oil or gas can be adequately
developed within the next twenty years except the nuclear.

7. Until the year 2000, only a combination of coal and nuclear
energy can satisfy the proper needs of the United States, according to

the definitive report of the National Research Council of the National Academy of Sciences.[4]

8. The same report estimates that by the year 2020 or 2030 the ratio of total energy use to Gross National Product can be cut in half if the country relies upon nuclear power.

9. All other industrial countries are surging ahead in the development of this power, including the use of the fast breeders with plutonium. There is a clear and unrelenting policy of the Soviet Union and the socialist countries of East Europe to magnify the nuclear capacity. The economic bloc, called Comecon, plans to increase the energy production from the present fifteen million to one hundred fifty million kilowatts by 1990.[5]

10. Developing countries want, and will increasingly need, nuclear power if they are to approximate their economic goals. Of course, the high costs and technical demands of constructing and maintaining nuclear plants will limit the number of such countries which are able to sustain them. Furthermore, this will imply a program of technical assistance by the more developed nuclear nations.

These ten points, expressed so briefly, may fail to convey the fact that they conceal a host of unresolved issues, even as they fail to demonstrate the extensive and costly ways by which data have been gathered and sifted in order to arrive at such generalizations. But they are recurring arguments in the expanding literature and in such public forums as the conference at M.I.T. They were cogently presented there by one of the World Council's leading consultants, M.I.T.'s own professor of nuclear energy, Dr. David J. Rose.[6]

Leading advocates of nuclear energy are not oblivious to the requirements for change which an expanded program will lay upon society. Such programs, in order to prove successful, will need to be carefully overseen by officials of government and private agencies, and with a continuity and consistency covering many years. As Dr. Alvin M. Weinberg of the Oak Ridge National Laboratory said in an oft-cited speech to the American Association for the Advancement of Science in 1971:

> We nuclear people have made a Faustian bargain with society. On the one hand, we offer—in the catalytic nuclear burner—an inexhaustible source of energy. . . . But the price that we demand of

society for this magical energy source is both a vigilance and a longevity of our social institutions that we are quite unaccustomed to.[7]

We note that in the conventional use of the analogy of Dr. Faust and Mephistopheles, the modern scientists are usually likened to Faust, and Satan is just himself, whereas Weinberg lets the nuclear physicists play the satanic role to society's Faust. To follow this comparison to its conclusion would lead to the time when the scientists would leer at society and say, "And now, at last, we claim your soul." But it is unlikely that Weinberg meant this. The uses of analogy have to be kept within reason. Even so, his emphasis on the continuing political and social implications of a thoroughgoing nuclear policy is realistic.

A Brief for the Anti-nuclear Position

1. The safety record of nuclear plants is already a dismal one. In many instances the accumulating corrosion in steam generators has caused plants to close for repair, having already allowed some radiation leakage. The plant at Three Mile Island near Harrisburg, Pennsylvania came to a full breakdown of operation in 1979; according to subsequent studies, it was on the brink of causing a genuine disaster. It is true that there have been no known fatalities from such events so far, but it is too early to learn whether radiation effects on persons will prove to have been harmful and even lethal. Meanwhile, unofficial but serious reports have told of two or three major accidents in the Soviet Union and two in Czechoslovakia, in at least one of which there were rumored fatalities of considerable number. The Communist press, as a matter of state policy, never reports such mishaps.[8] In any case, even if no catastrophe has happened yet, the potential for major disaster is present in each plant. Proponents fail to consider the primary factor which can cause major accidents, and that is human fallibility, both mental and physical. While machines may function as they should, the operators and attendants of a plant are susceptible to ignorance, misjudgment, carelessness, or just the stupefying boredom which the job entails. Garrett Hardin stresses this point forcibly.[9]

2. The safe and secure disposal of radioactive waste is so far from being realizable that utmost caution is needed to avoid adding further quantities of it. Salt mines and deep holes in the ground can leak and leach; steel containers eventually are eaten open by corrosion; concrete

161

cracks and decays. And radioactive material is always, in a sense, working for its own release. If the problem is already unmanageable, what would it be with thousands of plants in operation?

3. Is it a coincidence that plutonium is named for the god of the dead, ruler of Hades? Then Prometheus would recognize him in this element. This "miracle fuel" of the breeder reactor may not be harmful when contained with 100% surety, but it is an exceedingly dangerous radioactive poison with particularly easy access to the marrow of the bone, where only one-millionth of a gram suffices to initiate cancer. The policy statement of the National Council of Churches in the U.S.A. quotes the discoverer of plutonium, Dr. Glen Seaborg, as saying it is "fiendishly toxic." The statement continues:

> A small amount can produce cancer; it can also be used to fashion nuclear weapons. A plutonium-based economy will involve the handling and transporting of large amounts of plutonium. Because of the grave nature of the threat to life and world peace, a plutonium-based economy would require accident-free performance by machines and human beings. [Here citing Alvin M. Weinberg] Given these conditions, plutonium is not a fuel appropriate to the dimensions of human nature.[10]

To this policy statement, which the representatives of many American denominations adopted in May 1979 by a vote of 120 to 26, may be added the strong words of Dr. Jean Rossel at M.I.T.:

> The nuclear industry produces concentrations of artificial radio-activity which are several tens of millions greater than those existing in nature. Even if perfect and trouble free operation of atomic installations were to be assured, slow and steady pollution of the biosphere is inevitable in the generation of nuclear energy. . . . The assured protection of the biosphere against the infiltration of radioactive wastes for the next several thousand years is the most disturbing of the unsolved problems.[11]

4. The claim that atomic energy can be produced and delivered more cheaply than any other may be true, but it still should be questioned in the light of enormous repair and decommissioning costs, which consumers and taxpayers must bear.

5. Even given the present crisis of having no satisfactory and avail-

able alternative to the oil-gas economy, because of all the hazards of light-water and fast-breeder reactors, it would be wiser for a short time to revert to the use of coal, both for generators and for conversion to fuel oil. At the same time, there should be research and development, on a massive scale, of renewable resources, especially the solar. One thinks of the lunar landing project by NASA or the all-out effort during wartime as examples of how the political and technological power of the country can be mobilized for a single objective of highest significance.

6. There is apprehension over the inherent dangers in the corporate ownership of such a vast economic empire as nuclear energy would certainly become, especially in the United States. In most other countries it would be owned by the people through their government. In either case, however, it would bring about more and more concentration of great and decisive power in the hands of relatively few persons. The analogies already exist in the form of transnational corporations and cartels which control petroleum products.

7. Nuclear protagonists admit that the domestic and military uses of energy cannot be kept wholly apart. While they advance the argument that this connection will, in any case, be determined by political powers, rather than by the participatory voices of the citizenry, they minimize unrealistically the way in which the proliferation of domestic nuclear production will inevitably contribute to the growth of military might. For this very reason, in 1978, France broke its agreement with Pakistan and refused to deliver a nuclear energy plant. Moreover, considering the strategic importance of the plants and the huge number of them which are intended, they would become prime targets for sabotage and bombing. The possible peace of the world will come by reducing nuclear capabilities rather than by multiplying them.[12]

8. Related to the military dangers are those of political terrorism. The experiences of the past decade show the impossibility of preventing dreadful acts of slaughter, capturing jet planes, and bombing buildings. These atrocities would certainly be escalated in destructiveness and horror with the increase of nuclear plants. In particular, since it would be most improbable that any security system could prevent absolutely the theft of plutonium (five kilograms of which are sufficient

to make a kiloton bomb), the existence of breeder reactors would literally play into the hands of irrepressible terrorists.

9. The ninth and last counter against nuclear advocacy has to do with the poorer and newly developing nations of the two-thirds of humanity. Opinions are divided on this. There is no hesitation about wanting to see these people and nations bring their economic production to ever higher levels, and it is indisputable that a sufficient energy supply is indispensable for economic growth. By and large, as Dr. Benjamin Nwosu of the Nigerian Ministry of Education has often asserted in World Council of Churches meetings, they want nothing of Schumacher's "small is beautiful" theory.[13] Big countries such as India, Brazil, and Nigeria need big production, and energy is one of the keys to it. But is nuclear energy appropriate to most developing countries? That question has to be raised country by country. And the answer is seen to be negative by opponents of nuclear power.

So go the continuing debates.

RESOLVED: *That our country should adopt a policy of fully developing nuclear energy.* That would be a fitting topic for high school debating teams, and no doubt it is presently being used in such competition. The nineteen points sketched above could be very useful. The students would find them instructive.

When men and women in high places of responsibility carry on the same debate, however, they do not consider it to be rhetorical sport. It is their task to understand the issues in all their complexity, and then to offer counsel to the final makers of policy, or to make such decisions when they are the ones so authorized. One does not need to reiterate the plain truth that a country's energy decision at this time is of the highest importance for millions of people during the years ahead. Once the course has been chosen, there is to be no turning back, but only some modifying of direction or pace of development.

SCIENCE AND FAITH INTERACT

Only a few of the men and women engaged in discussions within the churches and councils of churches belong to the small circles of corporate and national decision-makers. They are obviously not of that all too common view which holds that the churches have no business meddling in public affairs, but could use their energy more effectively in praying and preaching the Gospel. They know that in this instance the churches have truly "done their homework" on all aspects of the problem, and that they have some wisdom to contribute which might come from no other source. This was signally recognized in 1977 when the World Council of Churches study became a major component of the United Nations' International Conference on Nuclear Power and Its Fuel Cycle. Planned by the International Atomic Energy Agency and held in Salzburg, the event drew two thousand scientists as participants. A whole session was given over to the Council's presentation, and Dr. Abrecht was then invited to chair the meeting.

In this unique setting, the Council's insights were presented by Dr. John Francis, an Anglican layman and research fellow in energy studies in Scotland. To the well-informed body he did not lay out all the pros and cons, but gave the following digest of the Church and Society commission's findings:

> Nuclear energy offers the potential of providing a large part of the world's energy needs, counterbalanced by some exceptional risks. It would be politically naive to think that nuclear energy will or can be abandoned.

> The maturity of the nuclear energy system is not yet such as to justify large-scale, or unlimited application; the consequences of further large-scale dependence need to be assessed.

> The right of access to nuclear technology must be recognized; the nuclear "haves" should not deny the nuclear "have nots" by any form of exclusive consultation.

> The issues of access and security involve the collective responsibility of all nations which needs to be assessed anew through the IAEA, with more clearly defined functional objectives appropriate to the anticipated scale of the task.

> Public confidence in the use of nuclear energy, seriously shaken in recent years, can be revived only by the widest possible public discussion of the technical options and of the value judgments underlying the present patterns of energy consumption.

Left unexpressed in this presentation, but underlying them, were

165

some of the concerns of the ecumenical consideration. These include the human feelings of moral obligation, the kinds of societies we wish to have in differing countries, the voluntary restraints which will be necessary for enhancing the lives of the greatest number of people, and the role of energy decisions in the purposes of history as understood in biblical and religious teachings.

The difference between a secular-scientific approach to energy and a religiously-informed one is not that the former is factual and realistic while the latter is theoretical and idealistic (both have to share the same factual and technical data). But the latter, needing no esoteric language of the Bible or theology, can fill such words as justice, participation, and sustainability with meanings which come from the treasury of Christian understanding of life in God's creation and according to God's will. In this interaction, the views on energy which are informed by the presuppositions of faith are critically influenced by the knowledge and interpretations of scientists and engineers; reciprocally, the religious insights are offered as valuable but easily ignored aspects of the total problem.

The contrast is illustrated, as is the need for interaction, by two statements within longer analyses of energy resources. First is the Council's statement of 1978. It concludes with expressions of concern for "the vast inequalities in access to energy, both within most societies and between the rich and poor societies of the world. The sharing of resources is a moral demand." It also emphasizes the need of people generally to "share in the decisions that affect their lives." And the report concludes with the plea, "Perhaps the most morally demanding foresight is that involved in concern for future generations, whom we can heedlessly imperil by exhaustion of resources that they will need."[15]

The second document is the authoritative seven hundred page report on "Nuclear and Alternate Energy Systems" by the National Research Council of the National Academy of Sciences. It concludes its recommendations for the nation's transition within fifty years to an almost totally nuclear energy system (with whatever effective sources can also be developed in that time) by observing: "The question is whether we are diligent, clever and lucky enough to make this inevitable transition an orderly and smooth one."[16] There is no mention of the elements of human justice within or beyond the country, of the perceived good of the citizenry, or of resources for future generations. It says only that there will be "large social and political components" and an "irreducible element of conflicting values and political interests." In short, the moral dimension was barely alluded to, except as being an area of probable conflict.

The two kinds of inquiry do obviously need each other. And it is at least of interest to note that in this case their bridge of interaction is Professor David J. Rose, who has taken part in both studies.

Where the Academy's report commends diligence and luck, the Council's could speak of faithfulness and resolute action.

IS THE WARNING
"USE LESS!" USELESS?

In this whole debate, all persons seems to agree on one conclusion, even though with differing ideas of what it requires. That is conservation. It is the word and the mandate which more than others tests whether *we* have the energy, or whether we only seek the *energy*.

In all the questing for alternative ways of providing fuel and power, the first result is recognition of the primacy of thoroughgoing conservation. The report of the group project of the Harvard Business School, *Energy Future,* made it utterly plain that this is the first and best option.[17]

As other investigators have done, the Harvard team considered all the possible options in addition to oil, gas, and nuclear energy.

Coal comes first to one's mind. It will certainly be used a great deal more than in recent years. But to make the burning of it conform to minimum standards of environmental protection, much care and expense will be incurred to scrub the coal for firing in more efficient furnaces. Otherwise, the air will become heavily laden with sulfurous wastes and carbon dioxide along with other deleterious chemicals. Not only would these chemicals cause respiratory distress for many people —as they do now in China and East Europe, and as they used to do in England—but the incremental rate of carbon dioxide would undoubtedly build up to the level of irreversible danger to the earth's whole biosphere. More imminently, with the increase of coal production would come more and more pulmonary and cancerous illnesses of coal

167

miners, as well as severe and fatal accidents in the mines. Coal is abundant and must be used, but with caution in the face of unavoidable dangers.

Thermonuclear fusion, as distinct from fission, is one of the most appealing processes for gaining endless energy. The most recent research and experimentation with models is promising, but its general availability may first be enjoyed by people two or three generations hence.

Solar energy is more attractive than any, indeed dazzlingly so. Not only the constant rays of the sun's radiant warmth, but its direct products—that is, every kind of plant—can be used. Newly invented devices and systems for heating water and warming houses are growing in popularity; but their high cost is still a hindrance to wide-scale conversion of heating systems. Even so, the concept is intriguing. Sunlight is clean: it purifies rather than pollutes. And it is free for everyone. As Jesus taught, God "makes his sun to shine on the evil and on the good," with no national, racial, or economic discrimination. For the capturing of volumes of solar energy sufficient to assist in a nation's total need, however, an all-out effort will have to be made. Theoretically feasible are the plans for immense photovoltaic structures for the immediate conversion of sunlight to electrical energy. Huge reflecting mirrors would focus the rays on "towers of power" which would receive the transmitted heat and operate generators. Having reached the moon, can we also yoke the sun?

Biomass is a real option to which we are beginning to awaken. Utterly immense quantities of vegetable matter are growing every second of time, on land and in water, by the plants' trick of photosynthesis, using carbon dioxide and water with chlorophyll. From small weeds to agricultural waste to windfall trees there are countless tons of biomass which can be efficiently oxidized rather than wasted. However, the maintenance of delicate ecological balances requires wise caution in the consumption of biomass for fuel.

There is also biogas, derived from digested solar food products in the animals and humans which eat them. It has been demonstrated in India that rural village needs for both fertilizer and fuel (methane) can be supplied by modest conversion plants using human and bovine excreta.[18]

Geothermal energy comes from hot springs, geysers, and apertures of the earth in volcanic areas.

Winds can still be captured and tamed at varying velocities short of tornadoes and hurricanes by modern improvements on the traditional windmill.

In short, apart from fossil fuels and nuclear energy, the earth is always transmitting inestimable powers. We see them flow and feel them blow. But only in delimited geographical areas can these natural powers be utilized for generating electricity and meeting a small fraction of the total energy requirement.

What is the sum of all these alternatives when they are added? After considering the lesser options with the greater, from biogas to coal and nuclear fission, the experts assure us that the one immediate priority is still conservation. After that, in order of importance but not in time sequence, come the research and development in the best uses of the major sources.

Conservation should not be considered only a negative factor: that is, just our not consuming a quantity of fuel. It is a positive way of meeting energy needs and also of enhancing the flagging sense of human mutuality and responsibility. The old, preinflation adage, "A penny saved is a penny earned," applies also to millions of barrels of oil and tons of coal. There are two distinct ways of understanding this, and a full effort of conservation will embrace both. One is just the elimination of waste. The other is the planned reduction of consumption of what have been thought to be essential materials and commodities. The first requires intelligence, ingenuity, prudence, diligence; the latter, the moral courage of self-restraint.

Careless, spendthrift people want to pay no attention to either mandate. Foolishly, they will go on wasting energy and material goods. Selfishly, they will acquire, possess, and consume all they can for their own indulgence and gratification. Individual persons are of that disposition, but so are entire segments of human society. The energy shortage is challenging individuals and the whole of society at once.

Acts of conservation by individual persons and families may seem trivial in relation to the national and global scope of the problem. If a conserving effort can save one's own money, fine! But a sense of responsibility often ends with the personal or family budget. As the pinch continues to become more distressing, and the costs of fuel and electricity keep increasing along with the prices of myriad consumer products which depend on them, people will realize that individual acts of conservation belong to the total effort of society. Barring sheer stupidity as well as perverse disregard for people's well-being, many citizens will have their automobile engines tuned for efficiency and drive more slowly, as smaller cars become more plentiful. They will reduce the use of fuel and electricity in their homes and preserve usable waste for recycling. These are, in fact, highly important actions of small-scale conservation. They include a psychological and moral dimension which anyone can perceive and feel: namely, a person's sense of doing something worthwhile for the whole community—"doing my bit." In addition, there is a religious dimension for those who are sensitive to implications of belief in God as the creator. It is the double satisfaction of using the earth's resources, even in smallest degree, with a sense of stewardship and thankfulness, and at the same time conserving what may be needed and used by people who are deprived and poor. The fact that these are simple, undialectical, old-fashioned virtues does not dilute their significance for today.

The major measures of conservation must rely on more than the personal virtues, however. Under national programs, both incentives and penalties are required: for example, tax benefits for home and apartment owners who install insulation and for industries which introduce energy-saving methods; penalties in the form of stiff fines for violating codes of construction and environmental protection. A massive reconception and reordering of America's public transportation system is obviously and painfully urgent, after decades of gross neglect of it in favor of highways for private cars and commercial trucks. The entire automobile industry will be further modified, as the car is "reinvented" for fuel economy. This agenda can be extended, as is already well understood. In short, conservation in the full twofold sense means a radical and discomforting change in our accepted ways of living in a prosperous technological society.

A NEW KIND OF HUMAN SOCIETY

Permeating the whole ecumenical inquiry and debate on energy is this deep-probing question of what may loosely be called the values of living. The presentiment grows that in this technological civilization the time has arrived for habits of living to catch up with the new scientific era. It is to be expected that there must be a time lag. Only about a quarter of a century, a mere generation, has passed since the commencement of the three new scientific eras: atomic, cybernetic, and microbiological. The pessimistic critics of technology may deplore these events and trends, but they are here to stay and will continue in development. Men and women and (especially) children are becoming accommodated to the changes. Is it not reasonable to claim that the post-1973 fuel crisis has suddenly galvanized whole populations into making adjustments more rapidly? And they do so in cognizance of the fact that the world of technology is at the same time a world of increasing population density and decreasing natural resources.

Contrary to one popularly held but dreaded notion, this accommodation to both technological mastery and energy deficiency must not be allowed to take an Orwellian shape, where people become automata in servitude to the mass society. This admonition applies not only to a total state but to a cultural conformity to George Orwell's "right think" in all matters where taste, style, education, morality, and human relations are concerned. In rich countries, this conformity, subtly disguised as freedom, would be to patterns of greed, acquisitiveness, consumerism and disregard for anyone else. In poorer lands, it would mean regimentation of the poor and weak by an oligarchy committed to its own lust for power. It is a melancholy fact that evidences of such trends in both directions are abundant. In either case, the benefits of energy systems would serve the powerful and be withheld from the weak.

The witness of the churches is to the other kind of future. There is an armamentarium of the churches which, for all its latent power, is easily and often neglected. It does not consist of a superior knowledge of economics, technology, and social forces; neither is it a monopoly on human sympathy and moral rectitude. Persons representing the churches' concern for energy and a livable society are sharers with others of differing religions, ideologies, or humanistic views in the possession of both empirical and theoretical knowledge and moral sensitivity. They must not permit the false impression to be disseminated that the churches can arrogate to themselves the resolution of these awesome problems. As sharers with humanity, however, the churches may testify to a particular regard for the just distribution of the goods

171

of the earth among the least advantaged people who make up the majority; to respect for the dignity and freedom of all persons who, as God's own creatures, are infinitely precious; and to faith that the seeming terrors of an unpredictable future can be replaced by hope for a good, genuinely human life for all.

Such faith and hope are posited on a different kind of energy. The Greek theologians call it the *energeia* of God. It is the spiritual power by which the Creator sustains all things of the universe in their ordered ways, and also leads a reluctant, halting humanity to accept that same *energeia* in their personal and communal existence. The manifestation of divine energy in human life is the unsentimental, potent quality of love. Upon critical analysis and exploration of its possibilities, the energy of love can be found to be the driving power of humanity, both in the least as well as the most technologically developed societies.

NOTES

1. E. F. Schumacher, "Implications of the Limits to Growth Debate: Small Is Beautiful," *Anticipation,* 13 (December 1972): 14.

2. John Francis and Paul Abrecht, eds., *Facing Up to Nuclear Power* (Philadelphia: Westminster Press, 1976), pp. 5–19. This book consists of articles drawn from *Anticipation,* 20 and 21 (May, October 1975).

3. Paul Abrecht, ed., *Faith, Science and the Future* (Geneva: World Council of Churches, 1978), p. 70; also published by Fortress Press, Philadelphia, 1979.

4. Committee on Nuclear and Alternative Energy Systems, National Research Council, *Energy in Transition, 1985–2010, Final Report* (San Francisco: W. H. Freeman, 1980).

5. Eric Morgenthaler, "Soviet Bloc Is Pushing Nuclear-Power Plants even as U.S. Pulls Back," *The Wall Street Journal,* January 4, 1980, p. 1.

6. David J. Rose, "Toward a Sustainable Energy Future," *Faith and Science in an Unjust World,* vol. 1 (Philadelphia: Fortress Press, 1980), pp. 241–53.

7. Alvin M. Weinberg, "Social Institutions and Nuclear Energy," Francis and Abrecht, *Facing Up to the Nuclear Power,* p. 35. A republished version of the article in *Science,* 176 (July 2, 1972).

8. Eric Morgenthaler, "Soviet Bloc Pushing Nuclear Power Plants."

9. Garrett Hardin, "The Fallibility Factor," Francis and Abrecht, *Facing Up to Nuclear Power,* pp. 20–23.

10. "The Ethical Implications of Energy Production and Use," draft

of November 1978, National Council of the Churches of Christ in the U.S.A.

11. Jean Rossel, "The Social Risks of Large–Scale Nuclear Energy Programs," *Faith and Science,* vol. 1, p. 255.

12. See the discussion of military dangers of breeder reactors in *Anticipation,* 26 (June 1979): 39–40.

13. Benjamin Nwosu, "Quality of Life and Technological Options: The African Perspective," *Anticipation,* 17 (May 1974): 35.

14. *Anticipation,* 24 (November 1977): 5.

15. "Statement by the Working Committee of Church and Society," *Anticipation,* 26 (June 1979): 52.

16. National Research Council, *Energy in Transition, 1985–2010,* p. 72.

17. Daniel Yergin and Robert Stobaugh, *Energy Future,* Report of the Energy Project of the Harvard Business School (Cambridge: Harvard University Press, 1979).

18. A. K. N. Reddy, "Technology and Self-Reliance," *Anticipation,* 23 (November 1976): 27–29.